C000114562

Philip Oltermann was born i
moved to England when he
study English and German
and University College London. He
his family. As a journalist he has written for *Granta*, the
London Review of Books and the *Guardian*, for whom he is the
Berlin Bureau Chief. He is the author of *Keeping Up with the
Germans* (2012) and tweets at @philipoltermann.

Further praise for *The Stasi Poetry Circle*:

'[A] remarkable story . . . A terrific piece of reporting, full of
lively writing, gentle humour and delicate literary criticism. It
conjures up the petty rivalries, monstrous paranoia and small
pleasures of the GDR through the eyes of the poets without
losing its sense of irony and distance. The story weaves neatly in and out of the history of the GDR . . . A gorgeous and
moving story of the irrepressible richness of poetry.' Oliver
Moody, *The Times*

'It sounds like a movie script but somehow it's true . . . Warm,
vivid and touching.' *Sunday Times*

'Oltermann's erudite unpacking of their literary offerings . . .
sets his poets in the wider context beautifully, adding an unexpected piece to the puzzle of what made the East German
dictatorship and its citizens tick.' Hester Vaizey, *BBC History
Magazine*

'Gripping and highly readable . . . What makes this book so fascinating is the lives of its characters.' Daniel Johnson, *Literary Review*

'A magnificent book. I could not put it down. It is at once touching, exquisite, devastating and extraordinary – wonderful narrative, impeccable detective work, beautifully written. It manages to be understated and thrilling, a kind of literary page-turner.' Phillipe Sands, author of *East West Street*

'Philip Oltermann's chipper, nightmarish *The Stasi Poetry Circle* outlines the workings of totalitarianism with a plot worthy of Monty Python. A vivid, funny, and imperturbable portrait of Soviet Russia's most loyal satellite.' Nell Zink

---

by the same author

Keeping Up with the Germans

PHILIP OLTERMANN

THE STASI
POETRY CIRCLE

The Creative Writing Class

That Tried to Win the Cold War

faber

First published in 2022
by Faber & Faber Limited
Bloomsbury House
74–77 Great Russell Street
London WC1B 3DA

This paperback edition first published in 2023

Typeset by Paul Baillie-Lane
Printed and bound by CPI Group (UK) Ltd, Croydon, CR0 4YY

A CIP record for this book
is available from the British Library

ISBN 978-0-571-33120-8

MIX
Paper | Supporting
responsible forestry
FSC® C171272

Printed and bound in the UK on FSC paper in line with our continuing
commitment to ethical business practices, sustainability and the environment.
For further information see faber.co.uk/environmental-policy

2 4 6 8 10 9 7 5 3 1

For A. & E.

CONTENTS

THE CIRCLE (AND OTHER POETS)

Jürgen Polinske, Stasi Main Division VI: Passport Control,
surveillance of tourists
A border guard

Björn Vogel, Stasi Records Department Division XII: Central
Information Service and Archive
A second lieutenant

Rolf-Dieter Melis, Stasi Paramilitary Section: Guards Regiment
A major

Alexander Ruika, Stasi Paramilitary Section: Guards Regiment
A conscripted soldier

Gerd Knauer, Stasi Propaganda Unit: Working Group Public
Liaisons
A junior officer

Uwe Berger, Working Circle of Writing Chekists
A professional poet and leader of the Stasi poetry circle

Annegret Gollin, target of Operation 'Transit'
An unpublished poet and 'negative-decadent' citizen

Gert Neumann, target of Operation 'Anthologie'
A published novelist and member of the 'literary underground'

Although the characters in this book are real, some names have
been changed.

Lesson 1

PRELUDE

An introductory performance, action, or event preceding
and preparing for the principal or a more important matter.

As a new chill descended on Europe, Jürgen Polinske was waiting at the gates of the compound, thinking about ice cream. There was a place in Prenzlauer Berg he liked that sold chocolate, vanilla and changing fruit flavours at fifty *Pfennig* a cone. He'd been to ice cream parlours in Leipzig and Halle where they sold as many as twenty different flavours. Not Italian gelato like they had in the West, but good ice cream still. Creamy. His favourite was the simple, plastic-wrapped 'Moscow-style' ice cream you could buy at every corner store: exquisitely soft vanilla, between two sheets of waffle. Polinske belonged to an elite of connoisseurs who loved eating ice cream even when it was cold outside.

He rang the bell for a second time and checked his watch. He could see that his predicament was not without irony. As a member of the German Democratic Republic's Passport Control Unit, it was usually him who enjoyed taking his time to scrutinise the wads of permits and identification papers as the queues built up outside his checkpoint. Today the tables had been turned on him. Here at Adlershof, only the uniformed members of East Germany's paramilitary unit, the *Wachregiment* with their Bordeaux-red collar patches, were allowed to walk straight through the checkpoint. Plain-clothes members of the Stasi's other units had to bide their time after handing over their passports. The guard at the front desk made a call to the control room, who sent down a courier to pick

3

up the ID to take it back upstairs, where someone else checked it
against the daily list of accredited names.

But Polinske, a stocky man with restless eyes, was the last person
who would lose his cool over such games. What had nine years in
the army taught him if not how to stand and wait without losing
your temper? For the officers' exam he was hoping to take in a few
years' time, they apparently made you sit, back straight, for two
hours, no fidgeting allowed. Well, they could bring it on. Before he
was moved to the border checkpoint at Friedrichstrasse, Polinske
used to stand guard at munitions points: stupid, mind-numbing
work, because you knew nothing would happen. Private citizens
weren't allowed to own guns anyway, so why would they come
thieving bullets? Yet if you were caught reading, listening to the
radio, writing or drawing or even just taking a leak, you'd be in
trouble. All you were allowed to do was scan the vista in front of
you: foreground, middle distance and background, from right to
left and from front to back. And then start all over again. So the
trick was to learn to entertain yourself using only your imagination. In his cadre file, Polinske's superiors sometimes bemoaned
his 'casual manners', his 'careless approach to working hours'.
'What he needs is self-control, to avoid drifting from a task set
to him and getting distracted by trivialities,' one report said. 'A
little bit more concentration will surely help him overcome this
weakness.' Turned out, they had it the wrong way around. Less
concentration is what he needed. Polinske had ended up a good
border guard because he was a good dreamer. And here he was,
standing outside the most heavily guarded military unit in East
Berlin, dreaming of ice cream.

The gate buzzed. A crackle on the intercom. 'Seminar room three,
on the first floor.'

The Adlershof compound was a mythical place in East Germany's imagination: the home of the GDR's elite fighting force, the Guards Regiment, the men who had supervised the building of the Berlin Wall. On maps of Berlin you could buy in the shops, the site was only a blank spot, without a description. If there had been text, it would have read: *Wachregiment* Feliks Dzerzhinsky, after the man who founded the Soviet Union's secret police and masterminded the mass executions of the Red Terror. According to the treaties drawn up by the four Allied powers, West Berlin was a 'demilitarised free city', without an army garrison and without conscription for men registered here: the city in which the capitalist and the communist worlds directly rubbed up against one another could not afford to have open explosives lying around in case the friction sent a rogue spark flying. As a result, West Berlin had over the course of thirty years amassed an army only of pacifists, drop-outs and dreamers as West Germans keen to avoid military service moved to the pre-war capital. Within the fortifications of the Adlershof military compound on the Eastern side of the Wall, however, those stipulations did not apply. In order to minimise its inhabitants' contact with the outside world, their compound contained all the amenities of a small village: there was a bank, a boot-maker, a bookshop, a radio station, a cinema, even a swimming pool with a diving facility. And even if these days their day-to-day duties were relatively mundane – protecting government apparatchiks at official functions, guarding state buildings, motorcading state visitors from Schönefeld airport into central Berlin, or even just making up the numbers in the stands at home matches of Dynamo Berlin, the Stasi's own football team – they knew what they had to do in an emergency. The 11,000-strong special fighting force trained beyond the gates of Adlershof did not only have 'in-depth and applicable political ideological knowledge of Marxist–Leninist theory', according to an internal training manual. Each man could run and swim long distances, fight with or without a weapon to 'defend himself against enemy assaults, stun, kill, tie up, search and cart off the enemy'. They could move undetected through enemy territory, using disguises and a network of safe houses. They could operate cameras to record enemy movements and send messages to their superiors via codified or encrypted communication. They could break a wrist with a flick of their elbow, blind an attacker with a torch and split a skull with a spade. Even within the East German military, gun control was tight; only a handful of officers had keys to the compound's arsenal. But if the Cold War turned hot, the well-drilled staff at the *Wachregiment* would know how to arm themselves in their sleep. Resting on wooden pallets in the long cellar rooms underneath the barrack buildings were crates full of hand grenades, bullets for the KK-MPi-69 – East Germany's own small-calibre Kalashnikov machine guns – and rocket-propelled grenades for anti-tank weapons. On sturdy shelves squatted twelve heavy Goryunov machine guns that could be mounted on armoured vehicles, as well as lighter Degtyarov guns, nicknamed 'record players' after their disc-shaped pan magazines. Specially made transport containers held semi-automatic carbines and officers' sabres; Makarov and Stechkin pistols were stored in a row of metal cabinets. The *Wachregiment* was poised for action.

But would that be enough? On this October day in 1982, even some members of the Ministry for State Security were not so sure. Once Polinske had been waved through at the gatekeeper's house, he took a sharp left and headed straight for a large rectangular building, standing at a right angle to the other barracks. On the corner, he passed a decommissioned Soviet tank repurposed as a war memorial, standing 2.45 metres high on a cordoned-off concrete plinth, bearing the number '09' and a large red star. The T-34 had once been the Soviet Union's *Wunderwaffe*, the secret weapon that turned the war against Hitler's army on the Eastern Front. Mass-produced in a remote site in Siberia, the agile and reliable armoured vehicle had outgunned German Panther panzers on the plains outside Stalingrad and chased the Nazis all the way back to Berlin. On 17 June 1953, Soviet T-34s had come thundering down the streets of East Berlin to help the *Wachregiment* quash a workers' uprising and protect their fledging socialist state. Three years later the T-34 rolled over the Hungarian revolution. In 1968 it crushed the Prague Spring. But in October 1982 the old Russian killing machine in Adlershof looked worryingly like a museum piece. Eleven months earlier President Ronald Reagan had reignited the arms race by passing a 197-billion-dollar defence appropriations bill, paving the way for a new range of high-tech weapons. They included the Rockwell B-1 Lancer supersonic bomber plane and the land-based LGM-118 MX (Missile, Experimental), dubbed the 'Peacekeeper' – an 'outrageous' name, wrote GDR newspaper *Neues Deutschland*, for a missile fitted with a 300-kiloton thermonuclear warhead. Reagan didn't want to hide his MX missiles underground like his predecessor Jimmy Carter, he wanted them positioned in missile silos in Arkansas, Kansas and Missouri, where they were ready to pounce. In February 1982 Reagan also ended a thirteen-year moratorium on chemical weapons: 155-millimetre artillery shells and 'Bigeye' aerial bombs would from now on be equipped with

lethal binary gases. It was a frightening arsenal, and one that the
Soviet Union, not to mention East Germany, looked incapable
of matching.

Polinske pushed open the double glass doors on the ground
floor and entered the foyer. In the summer, there had been a disciplinary procedure against the officer in charge of managing the
reception area. Bouquets of flowers had been ordered months
in advance, irrespective of whether they were required to greet
visiting dignitaries: a planned economy in miniature, but without the actual planning. Employees of the barracks' management
had made a habit of taking the surplus flowers home as gifts –
a novelty present for wives and mothers used to the carnations
ubiquitous in East German flower shops. A nice image: socialism
not just with a human face, but carrying a bunch of roses. But
this was a paramilitary compound. Were they meant to duel the
enemy with flowers? In Berlin's bars, a joke made the rounds in
those days. '*Wachregiment* Feliks Dzerzhinsky' was a misnomer, it
went: it should now be called '*Lachregiment Kirsch-Whiskey*', 'Joke
Regiment Cherry Whiskey'.

The smell of fresh floor polish wafted through the wood-panelled
foyer as Polinske traipsed up the stairs. As a standard security measure, the door of the seminar room had been secured like a medieval
scroll the previous evening. Before visitors were allowed to enter at
4 p.m., an officer had to remove the seal, a lump of putty embossed
with the regiment's signet, pressed into a piece of string hung
between the door and the door frame. The young border officer
surveyed the room as he took a seat. A portrait of the GDR's bespec-
tacled head of state, Erich Honecker, hung on one side of the room,
flanked by mock-crystal chandeliers. Vladimir Ilyich Lenin cast a
sceptical gaze from the wall opposite. Fifteen men had gathered

around a conference table, two thirds of them in their Dzerzhinsky uniforms, the other five in civilian clothing. Most of the group were under thirty, some of them teenagers straight out of school. On previous occasions, female members of the Ministry for State Security had attended the gathering, including a kitchen worker, but all the regulars in the group were male. Today they were all in attendance. Major Rolf-Dieter Melis, a thirty-eight-year-old veteran soldier and the most senior member of the circle. Björn Vogel, a thirty-three-year-old second lieutenant in the Stasi's central information service, with a strong stutter. Gerd Knauer, a slightly aloof junior officer in the propaganda unit, who was just about to turn thirty. And Alexander Ruika, a nineteen-year-old soldier doing his national service at the Erkner outpost.

A small reed of a man in his fifties, with a pointed nose and black spectacles, sat at the top of the table. As he opened his file, the room fell silent.

Liebe Mitstreiter, he said. Dear comrades in arms. Today we are going to learn about the sonnet.

Polinske's name had jumped out at me from page 54 of a little red booklet, a collection of poems published on the occasion of the GDR's thirty-fifth birthday in 1984. The title of the slim paperback, falling down the front page in curling calligraphic letters, was *Wir über uns*, 'We about us'. The subtitle read: 'Anthology of the Working Circle of Writing Chekists'. The Cheka – this much I knew – was the abbreviated nickname of the Soviet Union's secret police, the 'All-Russian Extraordinary Commission', on which East Germany had modelled its own state security organ:

the *Ministerium für Staatssicherheit*, better known as the Stasi. I had first read about this anthology in a 2006 article in the news magazine *Der Spiegel*, where it was fleetingly mentioned in a review of the film *The Lives of Others*. Germany's legendary secret police had over several decades run a secret programme in which it tried to train its spies in the refined art of verse. 'The Stasi, a Red poets' society?', the article said. 'Does it get any more insane than that?' What an absurd meeting of mindsets, I had thought at the time: one of the most brutal spy agencies in history on the one hand, the refined craft of lyrical verse on the other. A secret police synonymous with the suppression of free thought, and an art form through which men and women had for millennia expressed their innermost feelings and desires. What had attracted one to the other? I found a reprint of the original booklet online and ordered it on a whim. But it ended up unread on my bookshelf: it was a collector's item, a curio, rather than a book to be read and reread.

In the spring of 2015, however, I found myself flicking through its pages again. The year had got off to a bad start, my personal life was in turmoil and I was having doubts about the direction of my career. To stop myself from spiralling into self-pity, I signed up as a volunteer at a day centre for the elderly in Kings Cross, near my office in London. An email from the coordinator Abul arrived. He was pleased I was eager to help – but did I have any actual skills I could offer to the group? My card game was poor, my darts hand shaky, my guitar-playing rusty. Perhaps this was the time to establish whether a three-year literature degree could be put to practical use after all? In the coming weeks, I met up with a group of six pensioners every Thursday lunchtime for an hour, and read verse, sometimes our own efforts but mostly other people's:

Christina Rossetti's 'Goblin Market' (sometimes), William Blake's 'The Tyger' (often), and (over and over and over again) Pam Ayres' 'Oh, I Wish I'd Looked After Me Teeth'.

It was in those weeks that I started to think about the Working Circle of Writing Chekists again. I was even more intrigued by its very existence now. Iambic pentameters don't write themselves, and motivating people to turn up and participate in a regular poetry circle takes time and effort, as I was learning in a small back room on the ground floor of the Great Croft day centre. Abul had warned me to steer clear of poems about loss and death, and I had struck W. H. Auden's 'Funeral Blues' off my list early on. But Eileen could not get enough of Hilaire Belloc's 'Matilda Who Told Lies, and Was Burned to Death', and Dawn stamped her feet with joy when we read Dylan Thomas's line about 'rage, rage against the dying of the light'. The dynamics of the group were sometimes difficult to keep in check. John wrote his own poems and wanted to talk about metre, Joyce liked the Old Testament and poems about the devil, and Michael with the giant hands fell asleep at the start of every meeting and woke with a smile on his face at the end. I thought I had started my pensioners' circle because I wanted to do some good, to help other people, but I was starting to wonder if I had tricked myself: perhaps it was me who was seeking help, to bring some structure and meaning to my life. It is not only the meaning of a poem that can be oblique, but also its function. I wondered what had inspired the leadership of the Stasi to start its poetry circle. What value did a secret police so ruthless and efficient in its subjugation of the people of East Germany see in training its employees in this vaguest of disciplines, the 'art of substantiating shadows, and of lending existence to nothing', as Edmund Burke once wrote? Did spies need pastoral care? And if that was the stated aim, was it also the actual motive behind it?

The open tone of ice-cream-loving Jürgen Polinske's poems in the red booklet suggested he might be a good starting point for finding out more. His poem 'Come' is an outstretched hand in six stanzas, a poetic appeal for honest conversations among good comrades:

Come
Let us talk
set your world to right
Come
Let's have a chat
About my latest plight
Come
If you are down in the dumps.

I found the email address of a Jürgen Polinske who worked as an archivist at Berlin's Humboldt University, and he replied within a few hours. He was happy to meet up, he wrote, but 'how much time we will need will depend on your questions'. After the fall of the Wall, he explained, most of his former colleagues had had bad experiences with the press. We met on 28 August 2015, at a restaurant under the railway arches in Berlin's Mitte district, just down the road from Friedrichstrasse station where he used to wave people across the Iron Curtain. I nervously turned up fifteen minutes early and ordered the currywurst with potato salad. Polinske ambled into the restaurant on the dot, portlier than in the picture I had seen in his Stasi file, his dark brown hair now white and slightly curly. He ordered a cup of Earl Grey tea without milk.

Jürgen Polinske had slid into the Stasi sideways. He had started writing poems at school, but hadn't known how to turn his hobby into a profession. After eighteen months of compulsory military service, he had started studying crystallography at the Humboldt University, one of only two such undergraduate degrees in Europe at the time. But he had struggled with the physics components of his course, and was getting bad grades in maths too. After two years, someone from the Stasi turned up on his doorstep and asked whether he had considered going back into service. He enjoyed writing poems, didn't he? Then he could write reports too. And so he had ended up with the Passport Control Unit, which was formally integrated into the Ministry for State Security and therefore one up from the ordinary border patrols. First at Drewitz, near Potsdam, then at Friedrichstrasse station in the heart of the capital, known as the 'palace of tears' because of all the weepy goodbyes it has seen over the years. On one occasion a big lorry had come pelting past his checkpoint at full speed and he had yanked his Makarov out of its holster and pointed the gun up at the sky. The suspect driver had hit the brakes and Polinske and his colleagues had practically taken apart the entire vehicle. In the end it turned out the van was only delivering fresh bread rolls to the American garrison. But Polinske had done his job. The incident resulted in an unusually positive entry in his otherwise mediocre personnel file: for once, he had proven himself to be 'self-reliant, determined and reliable'.

What had the Stasi tried to achieve with its poetry programme, I asked Polinske. Was the idea to help East Germany's working-class warriors better understand the decadent bourgeois mind? He shook his head, while conceding that his knowledge of the inner workings of the secret police was limited. His memories of what happened in the circle were sometimes sketchy, and clouded by disappointment. His poems were technically accomplished, but they could verge on the whimsical. 'Change', one of the poems he read out to the group, contrasts childhood memories of joyfully splashing through the rain with the reality of military exercise, when 'every puddle is an annoyance'. That one didn't make the cut for the anthology. Polinske also wrote a dramatic monologue in Berlin dialect that rhymed *jedürft* with *jeschlürft*, and *uff* with *druff*. They hadn't liked that either, and said so. Many of the young soldiers who turned up to the Working Circle of Writing Chekists had left with tears in their eyes after being informed, in no uncertain terms, of the poor quality of their work. Polinske too had stopped going after a few months: he had recently become a father, and had to prioritise his new family and job. He reckoned the only reason that his poem 'Come' had made it into the red booklet was because the final line withdraws the invitation made in the rest of the poem:

Come ... but not just to complain
because then
you had better not come at all.

The reason he had joined the Stasi poetry circle, Polinske said, was simple: 'I was still a bit green back then, not to say naive: I had artistic ambitions, and I thought I could learn something from the real poets who ran the workshop.'

If I really wanted to understand why the Stasi had set up the circle and how they planned to use it, Polinske said, I should try to contact the circle's former artistic leader, the thin man with the thick glasses. He had instilled the group with a dogma: poetry had to rouse emotion and boost the hunger for victory in class warfare. The group's literary shepherd believed his flock should write poems that were like marching songs: distractions from the everyday hardship of military life that also focused the mind on the ideological goal on the horizon. He had drawn their attention to the 'Red Orchestra' group of anti-Nazi resistance fighters run by Harro Schulze-Boysen and Arvid Harnack, who had habitually started their meetings by reading each other poetry before segueing into Marxist philosophy. He had told them the story of the sculptor and resistance fighter Kurt Schumacher, who had continued to write poems in his prison cell until the day of his execution, holding his pen with tied hands. And the thin man with the thick glasses became very excited when he discovered young poets who shared this idea of poetry's purpose. Polinske remembered this very clearly, he said. There had been a soldier who joined at the same time as him, eighteen like himself, called Alexander Ruika. He had read his poem about the Red Army's cavalry. Polinske would never forget this poem, he said. He could still picture the scene: when the young Ruika had finished the last line, there had been a few minutes of complete silence. And then the thin man with the thick glasses had spoken up ceremonially, and said: 'What a talent.'

The name of the thin man with the thick glasses? He was called Uwe Berger.

I paid our bill. Outside the cafe, before we waved our goodbyes, Polinske said something to me that I couldn't quite make sense of at the time: 'The question mark at the end of a poem is worth a hundred times more than a full stop. I know that now, after thinking about it for a long time. But I didn't know that then.'

Lesson 2

SONNET

A fourteen-line poem with a variable rhyme scheme.
Literally a 'little song', the sonnet traditionally reflects upon
a single sentiment, such as love, with a clarification or 'turn'
of thought in its concluding lines.

Asking Uwe Berger about the real purpose of the Stasi poetry circle turned out to be difficult, because Uwe Berger had died in a
Berlin hospital on 16 February 2014. A request for an interview
with his widow went unanswered. But in the absence of the man
himself, there was his body of work, whose very volume suggested
an impressive literary figure. Judging by his bibliography, describ-
ing Uwe Berger as prolific would be an understatement. By 1982,
aged fifty-four, he had twenty published books to his name, an
average of one every sixteen months since his 1955 debut, *The
Acquiescence.* They included collections of poetry, essays, novels
and travel writing, all published by East Germany's most important publisher, Aufbau, where Berger also worked as an editor.
Throughout the 1970s, he was the most frequently published poet
in *Neues Deutschland*, the official newspaper of the ruling Socialist
Unity Party, which sold around a million copies every day. He was
twice awarded the Johannes R. Becher medal, handed down to
those artists who 'advanced socialist culture', and won the GDR's
National Prize for Literature in 1972. Regarded as a poet of literary
merit himself, Uwe Berger was also closely involved in the East
German institutions that judged and rewarded the literary merit
of others. From 1973 until 1989, he was a board member of the East

German Writers' Union, the best-funded institution of its kind in the world at the time, with a network of fifteen offices across the country and an annual budget of three million Ostmark for literary stipends. From 1982, he was vice-president of the East German Cultural Association, which its founder Johannes R. Becher had intended to become the 'intellectual and cultural parliament of our country'.

What made Berger's literary status remarkable is that he had managed to rise to a position of such power and influence without ever joining the Socialist Unity Party, the SED. A fusion of the Social Democratic and Communist parties enforced by the Soviet administration, the SED did not see itself as a political party in the conventional sense, but as an 'avant-garde of the proletariat': it existed beyond all checks and balances, commanding authority over the judiciary, executive and legislative, as well as the other pillars of public life, such as the media and trade unions. The Central Committee of what East Germans only referred to in the singular, 'The Party', was the most powerful body in the land, prescribing policies that the country's ministers had to follow, and the Central Committee's General Secretary was automatically the head of state. Being a Party member was more of a must than a boon for any citizen with ambitions to get on in life, be it by taking a senior position in their field of industry or pursuing a career in the sciences or humanities. Accordingly, the Party's membership had swelled to around two million by 1982, meaning roughly every sixth person over the age of eighteen was carrying the red Party book. And yet Uwe Berger was somehow not among them.

In his writing, Berger never made his reasons for declining to join the Party explicit, but there are hints that are insufficiently subtle to be missed. Born in 1928, the youngest of two boys in a bourgeois family of Huguenot stock, he was one of around 200,000 teenagers who were drafted into the Luftwaffe in the dying days of the Third Reich as auxiliary staff, or *Flakhelfer*. In January 1944, as RAF bombers descended on the German capital in the latest of Arthur 'Bomber' Harris's ultimately unsuccessful 'Battle of Berlin' campaigns, the aspiring poet was among a line of shivering fifteen-year-olds marching to an anti-aircraft position in Grossziethen, on the south-eastern outskirts of the city. A British air mine the size of a wardrobe dropped from the sky over their barracks and would have wiped out the entire platoon, had it not embedded itself in the surrounding sand wall. But in spite of the death and destruction around him, Berger could not get himself to hate the planes in the skies above, or so he later wrote in his memoir, *Path into Autumn*: having listened to the BBC at home, he knew of the suffering the Luftwaffe had caused in Coventry. The real enemy was not in the skies above but in his own ranks. On his first night in the barracks, the freezing new arrivals were doused in cold water by the older members of the Wehrmacht, and in the following weeks he continued to witness ritual humiliation and arbitrary flashes of violence. In early 1945, as his service on the anti-aircraft guns was coming to an end, he volunteered for the military navy – to avoid being drafted into the Waffen SS, as he later explained.

In West Germany, the *Flakhelfer* generation of teenagers who were sucked into the Nazi war machine as it was going through its death throes went on to make a lasting impact on the country's political and cultural life. Many of them, such as the long-time Foreign Minister Hans-Dietrich Genscher, the novelist Günter Grass, the philologist Walter Jens and the cabaret satirist Dieter Hildebrandt, went on to become passionate advocates for a more democratic West Germany, not just in private but in public. It was as if their complicity in the National Socialist war effort spurred them on belatedly to carry out the resistance work they failed to do in their teens. Having experienced despotism at first hand, many *Flakhelfer* made it their life's work to restrain political power, by tying it to a strong constitution and dispersing its central actors across federal institutions.

Did the trauma of 1944 leave a similar stain on Uwe Berger's conscience? Did it make him unable to join the rank and file of party politics? Many of his contemporaries were certainly left with that impression. A *Berliner Zeitung* profile of Berger from August 1965 portrayed him as a 'lone wolf', who 'did not find or seek a connection' – the 'connection' presumably being one to the Socialist Unity Party. The journalist and painter Marina Dost, who befriended Berger during a beach holiday in Usedom in 1983, recalled him telling her that his tumultuous 'inner life' had made it impossible for him to join the Party's youth wing, the Free Democratic Youth, straight after the war, and that he still dreamt of a 'third way' between socialism and capitalism. As origin stories go, it was one that made Berger's political awkwardness not just understandable but almost forgivable, even in a one-party state. A 1961 article in Berlin's *National Zeitung*, a conservative newspaper compliant with socialist censorship, reminded readers that Berger was part of the 'youngest generation that had consciously experienced the Second World War'. It claimed that 'the thorn within you' – the title of one of Berger's collections of poems – was 'a reminder, a warning, the ever-present question of where-from and where-to'. His childhood trauma meant that Berger was 'intrinsically linked to the growing and becoming of our German Democratic Republic'.

Berger carried out his mission as the living link to Germany's darkest hour with not just dignity, but also a humility that was unmissable to anyone who crossed his path. His sartorial style, judging from photographs in newspapers, was the opposite of flamboyant: those heavy black glasses, crouching on a long and narrow nose; a lean neck protruding from monochrome turtleneck jumpers. His chronically poor state of health, too, is visible in those photographs: having been ravaged by jaundice and hepatitis as a child, he continued to suffer from abdominal tuberculosis, atrophy of the liver and severe chest pains. But Berger was not one to seek out vices to distract from his many ailments. With his second wife Anneli, a doctor he had met when she cared for his first wife, Inge, as she was dying from cancer, Berger lived in a sparsely furnished apartment in Köpenick, near the river Spree. He did not drive a car, didn't even have a driving licence. Berger wrote his poems on a typewriter, even when computers became more readily available. His most extravagant hobby outside writing was a collection of rocks and minerals he had picked up on travels around the Soviet empire: a piece of porphyry from a dry river bed on the Tian Shan, a splinter of crystalline schist from the banks of Lake Baikal, a fossilised seashell from the collapsing cliff line on Hiddensee, a man-made racloir from a meadow's edge on Rügen, a core stone made of sandstone that a gas worker near Salzwedel had given him as a present, a smoothened hunk of jade he had purchased in Irkutsk. Among Berlin's well-oiled literary circles, Uwe Berger's monkish asceticism was the stuff of legend. His editor at Aufbau, who used to visit him in his apartment every Christmas, realised one year that the glass of schnapps they drank together always came from the same bottle on his kitchen shelf: in the twelve months between their meetings, Berger would not take as much as a sip.

Sobriety was not just the principle by which Uwe Berger lived his life, but also the central quality he sought to achieve in his art, and a standard by which he judged the art of others. 'The question we should ask ourselves', he told his fellow board members of the East German Writers' Union in 1973, 'is does the poem serve the truth or not'. He warned his fellow writers of the dangers of interpretation: a good poem was a poem in which the writer's intention was clear for everyone to see. A good poet spoke the truth and nothing but the truth.

———————

To fully understand Uwe Berger's sense of poetic mission, one needs to delve deeper into East Germany's cultural origins. The history of the GDR is a book usually read back to front. The final chapter of socialist East Germany and its most dramatic moments are well known: a state being drained of its citizens as thousands head over to the West, first via Hungary and eventually straight across the border in Berlin. Politicians who once sent fear into the hearts of their opponents fumble their lines as a regime's once famously efficient bureaucratic apparatus descends into chaos. The images that prevail are of the story's spectacular last scenes. Empty shelves in East Berlin supermarkets. Grey boulevards lined with concrete tower blocks, inhabited by a forlorn, ashen-faced people – suddenly electrified with life as they take their first steps into the West on the night of 9 November 1989. Dances of joy on top of the Wall. Holes chiselled into the concrete.

But when stories have such vivid endings, the opening chapters can pale into obscurity, to the extent that it is sometimes hard to tell where the tale truly starts: the more incontestable the ending, the more room for negotiating alternative beginnings. In the case of East Germany, one of these possible opening chapters makes for a marked contrast to the closing scenes. It tells of a country not yet drained of colour and aspiration, but brimming with utopian hope, feverish creative ambition and at times absurdly idealistic expectations. At its most creative, its most idealistic and most utopian, it was the story of a state committed to the idea that art brings out the best in people, and of the only country in the world that believed it could build a new political order from a poetic form.

That version of the story starts with a plane breaking through the smoke-filled sky above Berlin to land at Tempelhof airport, on an airstrip surrounded by smouldering black ruins. It's 8 June 1945, just over a month after Hitler's forces in the city have surrendered to the Soviet army. One of the passengers on the plane is Johannes R. Becher, a fifty-four-year-old Bavarian poet and recovering morphine addict who has spent the last twelve years in Russian exile due to his membership of the KPD, the German Communist Party. The barbarism of National Socialism, Becher believed, had been expressed most profoundly in its disdainful treatment of culture: the mocking of artists, the hounding of writers, the burning of books, an attitude best summed up by a line in a play by the Nazi poet laureate Hanns Johst, commonly misattributed to Hermann Göring: 'Whenever I hear the word culture, I unlock the safety catch on my Browning.' As Becher was being driven from the airport through the ravines of rubble, he decided that any effort to rebuild the country of his birth needed to put culture back at centre stage. Germany might have been bombed into submission, its defeat the greatest and most shameful in its history, but beneath the rubble Becher spied the seeds of a new and better country. The Germany of Goethe and Schiller, of the *Dichter und Denker*, of thinkers and poets, was still alive. In his youth, Becher had been an enthusiastic follower of expressionism, the German avant-garde movement that celebrated inner turmoil and dark emotions. By the time he landed in Berlin, he had renounced his youthful scribblings. But an infatuation with acts of artistic expression as earth-shattering moments of pathos continued to shape his growing interest in politics. 'It lives, lives amongst all of us,' he wrote of Germany's grand intellectual tradition. 'A different, secret Reich.'

In Britain, wartime Prime Minister Winston Churchill, recently relegated to the opposition benches, was following developments in Berlin's Soviet sector with increasing concern. Not just the defeated German capital, but also other great Eastern European cities like Warsaw, Prague and Budapest, he noted in his famous 'Sinews of Peace' speech in 1947, now 'lie in what I must call the Soviet sphere, and all are subject in one form or another, not only to Soviet influence but to a very high and, in some cases, increasing measure of control from Moscow.' But Becher was either confident or arrogant enough to believe that East Germany would not just become a vassal state of the Soviet Union, but a master of its own destiny. This, after all, was a country whose boundaries contained the cities of Weimar, Europe's cultural centre in the age of eighteenth-century classicism, Wittenberg, where Martin Luther had nailed his ninety-five theses to the door of the castle church and kick-started the age of Reformation, and Leipzig, home of the world's first daily newspaper. And German was the native language of Georg Wilhelm Friedrich Hegel, Friedrich Engels and Karl Marx – the very thinkers whose philosophy underpinned the world-view of revolutionary Russia. Reading Marx had convinced Becher that the true Germany, the Germany of *Kultur*, could only flourish under socialism. According to the main author of *The Communist Manifesto*, one of the real sources of all evil was not the bourgeoisie or their capital, but the division of labour that had come about as a result of their political system. Under capitalism, 'each man has a particular, exclusive sphere of activity which is forced upon him and from which he cannot escape': you were forced to be a hunter, a fisherman, a herdsman, a critic or an artist. Under communism, Marx predicted these divisions would eventually fall away, and 'each can become accomplished in any branch he wishes'. Society would regulate the general production, thus freeing the individual to do one thing today and another tomorrow, 'to hunt in the morning, fish in the afternoon, rear cattle in the evening, criticise after dinner, just as I have a mind, without ever becoming a hunter, fisherman, herdsman or critic'.

Johannes Becher had put his finger on one of the great promises of the new social order: that there would not be workers in one corner of society and intellectuals in the other, but only workers who wrote and writers who worked. He even had a name for this new model society: the *Literaturgesellschaft*, or 'literature society'. In a literature society, Becher argued, creative writing would not merely reflect social conditions, but shape them. Literature would not just serve politics or distract from it: it would be a central pillar of the new socialist state. This was because literature, and specifically poetry, was more than just words on a page. Poetry, he insisted, was 'the very definition of everything good and beautiful, of a more meaningful, humane form of living': it was 'a creative order, an elevated form of existence', the 'eternal self-transcendence of man'. Fighting for this ideal was why Becher had gone into politics. Plato had banished poets from his ideal republic, but the GDR would do the opposite. In East Germany literature

had to have a *Grossmachtstellung*, Becher insisted, the 'standing
of a great sovereign power'. In his essay, 'A Defence of Poetry', the
English Romantic poet Percy Bysshe Shelley had called poets 'the
unacknowledged legislators of the world'. If Becher had his way,
the GDR was going to be the first state in the history of mankind
to give them their due credit.

One particular form of poetry was meant to shepherd the citizens of the new East German state into utopia: the sonnet. For
Becher, the defining trait of the sonnet was not its particular length
of fourteen lines, its set rhyme scheme, as the Italians practised it,
or the use of the iambic pentameter, as Shakespeare had it. Instead,
Becher believed that sonnets structurally mirrored the Marxist
view of historical progress. Hegel, the nineteenth-century German
philosopher, had argued that history moves towards a higher
stage of freedom in a 'dialectical' fashion, which is to say it follows
the same non-linear three-step pattern as an argument: from an
idea, the thesis, to a contradiction of that idea, the antithesis, to
a solution that resolves the tension between these two ideas, the
synthesis. Karl Marx had picked up Hegel's idea and turned it on its
head: society would develop from a bourgeois order into a state of
communism by following the same pattern, but its progress would
be shaped not by ideas but by material realities. Dialectical materialism, or *Diamat*, became the official world-view of the Soviet
Union and its satellite states, its study an obligatory part of every
East German university degree. But the GDR's poetic state builder
– Johannes R. Becher, Culture Minister and member of the People's
Chamber – believed that the people of East Germany could be
trained in Hegel's 'rhythm of insight' in a less dogmatic fashion:
through poetry. 'The sonnet makes its content life's law of motion,'
he wrote in his essay, 'Philosophy of the Sonnet', 'which consists of

statement, contrast and resolution in a concluding statement, or in thesis, antithesis and synthesis.' The sonnet was the algorithm that would guide East Germany's population of nineteen million gently into freedom, an idea that Uwe Berger enthusiastically endorsed in his poem 'Succession':

Good it is to tell the people: this is right,
and thus you must act! Better still, to let them
recognise themselves what is right, so they desire
to play their part in the transformation, be what will become,
and through self-abdication learn the unlearnable,
that which they have long known but continue to experience anew,
vulnerable and needy, but more helpful and stronger
than those who are only beginning to discover themselves in themselves
but what is right? The truth that doesn't stand still,
the immovable, the law of progress.

So far, so utopian. However, Becher had a plan for what politics needed to do in order to bring about the impossible. He was a key member of the reformed German Communist Party in the Soviet occupied zone, and spent the next few years in a flurry of activity to achieve his dream. Becher founded the *Kulturbund*, a cultural association dedicated to the 'renewal of German culture', sending representatives to the lower house of the new East German parliament. He helped set up two literary journals to amplify the German voices returning from Nazi exile, and founded the Aufbau publishing house, which would start by publishing the books Hitler's cronies had burned in town squares. And he sat down with the composer Hanns Eisler – who had spent the war years exiled in the United States, like his former teacher, the great modernist,

Arnold Schoenberg – to write the GDR's national anthem, 'Risen from Ruins': a euphoric, chest-beating piece of music in comparison to the sombre anthem of West Germany.

Becher also made sure to approach some authors who looked 'politically unreliable' because they hadn't fallen foul of the Nazi censors. One of them was the bestselling novelist, Hans Fallada. Like Becher, Fallada was a recovering morphine addict, and the two men shared an unusual trauma from their teenage years: both were sole survivors of attempted double suicide pacts. Becher dropped in Fallada's lap a batch of Gestapo files outlining the story of Otto and Elise Hampel, a poorly educated, previously apolitical couple who spent nearly three years evading the Gestapo in order to leave handwritten cards with anti-Nazi messages around Berlin. They were eventually caught, and were executed at Plötzensee prison in Berlin in 1943. But Becher made sure to conceal the file containing the less than heroic episode in which the Hampels petitioned for mercy and accused each other of being the main instigator behind the postcard campaign. Ravaged by his morphine addiction but still miraculously productive, Fallada used the Hampels' story as the basis for a novel that would prove a bestseller for decades to come: *Jeder stirbt für sich allein*, or, to give it its later English title, *Alone in Berlin*. It was the kind of book that lived up to Becher's billing: a rousing historical tale that didn't just reflect the social conditions of its time, but had the power to shape them.

The Soviet administration, though suspicious of Becher's obsession with the grand German cultural tradition, put policies in place that helped him realise his plan. In the famine years immediately after the war, artists and actors were among the select few professional groups to whom the Russians supplied *payoks*, additional care packages containing meat, potatoes and sugar. After monetary reform in 1948, they would receive the same top-tier food vouchers as approved key workers such as roofers, miners and bricklayers. Writers returning from exile were given privileged access to building materials so they could renovate destroyed homes. Leading figures from the arts and sciences, such as the poet and dramatist Bertolt Brecht, were pampered with a reduced income tax rate, lifelong retirement pay and, in the early years, special shops catering only for the intelligentsia. Others were eventually promoted to posts in government: Alexander Abusch and Alexander Kurella, two other reformed expressionist poets, joined the Socialist Unity Party's Central Committee. Becher himself was appointed Minister for Culture in 1954. Even though Becher only served as a minister for four years, dying of cancer in October 1958, the GDR had by then begun to internalise his big idea. A month earlier at the annual Party conference, the president of the ruling Socialist Unity Party, Walter Ulbricht, had announced the measures he believed East Germany needed to take in order to surpass West Germany – not just in economic terms, but also in general quality of life. 'In our state and our economy, the GDR's working class has already taken charge,' Ulbricht said. 'Now we must also scale and seize the heights of culture.'

The term 'literature society' never found its way into official legislation, but it would rattle around politicians' heads for the next four decades: in 1981, General Secretary Erich Honecker still championed his state as a 'country of readers' – as opposed to what he called the 'bestseller country' on the other side of the Berlin Wall. Even after Becher's death, his utopian vision was welded into the self-image of this small country. In the 1970s, the government would still insist that the relatively small number of steady, regular readers of *schöne Literatur*, or high literature, represented a 'key problem'. A mere thirty-five per cent of the adult population reading Goethe and Pushkin was not enough: in East Germany, that number needed to go up to eighty-five to ninety per cent, and ideally within five years. Socialist men and women had to steel their brain and body with equal vigour. Theatres and opera houses handed out a proportion of their tickets to factories or educational institutions. A 1973 decree prescribed that larger factories must have an on-site library with five hundred to a thousand books, staffed by a part-time librarian. If the factory had over five hundred workers, the librarian needed to work full-time. Bigger factories needed more books, eighteen to thirty thousand of them in any enterprise employing between five and ten thousand employees.

Publishers, like their customers, had to adhere to the principles of the planned economy: in terms of books printed, the stated aim was a yearly increase in productivity of four to five per cent. Between 1950 and 1989, both the number of books printed per year and the proportion of those that were fiction more than tripled, even as the country's population declined. Even West German academics paid grudging respect: an average of six to nine books per head printed every year put little East Germany up at the top of the book production charts, alongside the Soviet Union and Japan. An International Study of Reading Literacy, conceived before the fall of the Wall but carried out just after, found that 'the average reading comprehension of East German eighth-graders was significantly higher than that of their West German contemporaries'. This didn't necessarily mean that socialist Germans automatically read more than capitalist Germans – or if they did, it doesn't show up in comparative surveys. But it did mean that East Germans read more closely: they excelled at working out not just what a text said on the surface, but what it said between the lines, irrespective of whether that text was a poem by Goethe, a newspaper article on the opening of a new chemical plant, or *The Communist Manifesto*. The Franco-American literary critic George Steiner, not a figure whose cultural observations could be accused of being clouded by political leanings, noted in his 1978 essay 'The Uncommon Reader' that the reading public east of the Iron Curtain had sustained a more intense, quasi-religious relationship with the written word. The Soviet Union, he pondered, was 'a society which is bookish in the root sense, which argues its destiny by perpetual reference to canonical texts'. And with a reading public so well trained in the art of exegesis, the GDR was a state in which even senior officials, bureaucrats and those working to protect the ruling system could not afford to ignore literature.

Becher's vision gave birth to one policy of particular relevance to the Chekists at the Adlershof compound, even if the man himself was no longer alive by the time it took shape. In April 1959, the Socialist Unity Party organised a conference with leading authors from around the country in the town of Bitterfeld, home to one of Europe's largest chemical complexes. The programme that emerged from this meeting became known as the 'Bitterfeld Path': in order to bridge the divide between the working classes and the intelligentsia, writers would be plucked from their bourgeois writing dens and placed amongst manual workers in factories or coal mines. The writers would work in the factories but also help run so-called 'Circles of Writing Workers', following the motto: 'Pick up the quill, comrade!' Within a few years, every branch of industry had its own writers' circle: train carriage construction workers, chemists, teachers. By the end of the GDR in 1989, there were still three hundred of them. For some of the more talented novelists recruited into the scheme, it kickstarted their careers and inspired their best works: Christa Wolf wrote her prize-winning novel, *Divided Heaven*, after her placement at a train wagon manufacturer; Brigitte Reimann penned her masterpiece of socialist realism, *Arrival in the Everyday*, while leading a circle at a brown coal mine; Erik Neutsch composed his bestselling nine-hundred-page novel, *Trace of Stones*, while he was amongst workers at a chemical plant.

East Germany's secret police did not wait long to get in on the act. The first passing references to 'Writing Chekists' in the Ministry for State Security appear in the files as early as 1960. In 1961, the Stasi's administrative branch in Berlin records a second 'lyrical evening', attended by three of its full-time employees. For the next two decades, the intelligence agency's dedication to lyrical praxis was sporadic, with a group of operatives sitting down to compose the words for a festive march in 1968, and a poetry workshop on the occasion of the GDR's twenty-second anniversary in 1971. Then, for reasons that are still unclear, the Stasi decided in the late seventies that it needed to professionalise the work of the Circle of Writing Chekists: in terms of quality, an internal report noted, there had been a 'discrepancy between aspiration and reality'. Ulrich Grasnick, a poet renowned for his collaboration with the painter Marc Chagall, was informally approached about the possibility of leading the group, but found a way to excuse himself. Some time in spring 1982 (the precise date of the approach is unclear from the files), the Stasi put out feelers to Uwe Berger, the ascetic without a Party membership but a firm believer in poetry's truthfulness. Berger accepted.

Lesson 3

CONSONANCE

The repetition of identical or similar consonants in
neighbouring words whose vowel sounds are different.

Under Berger's tutelage, a new discipline descended upon the
group. Meetings were held at regular intervals, always in the same
room, and they started on time: once every four weeks, the group
gathered at 4 p.m. for two hours in the room on the first floor of
the *Kulturhaus*, the House of Culture inside the Adlershof compound. Stasi members from branches outside the regiment needed
to request an invitation before they could drop by. Young soldiers
who were doing their three-year military service in the Guards
Regiment had to wear their uniforms; officers could attend in civilian clothing. After initially being addressed with the formal *Sie*,
the group's leader had offered the Writing Chekists the informal
du, though occasionally, in moments when the student-teacher
hierarchy was hard to ignore, the group would slip back into the
polite mode of addressing each other.

Lessons had a clearer structure under Berger. Members of the
programme were required to take turns reading out poems they
had written in their spare time. Berger asked the rest of the group
what they made of each poem, encouraging a discussion. Only
once this discussion had finished did he himself comment on
the technical aspects of the work, always in a polite voice, rarely
overtly critical. Did they know what an iambic pentameter was? A
Petrarchan sonnet had two stanzas, an octave with eight lines and
a sestet with six. A rondel consisted of two quatrains followed by

a quintet or a sestet. A villanelle had five tercets and a quatrain. A rhyme alone didn't make a poem. The judge of a rhyme, Berger told them, was the ear and not the eye. If you put a cross rhyme into the first four lines – abab – then you also had to put a cross into the next four: cdcd.

In terms of literary merit, it soon emerged, the group had a mountain to climb. The soldiers in their late teens in particular had an irresistible urge to pen love poetry that paid little attention to political debates. In the early years of the Stasi poetry circle, this was tolerated. One young member of the secret police fantasised in free verse about being kissed by a young maiden who was unaware of his lowly rank, thus elevating him to a 'lance corporal of love'. 'Patiently I wait', the lusty teenager wrote, 'for my next promotion / at least / to general'. Another young soldier imagined in a sestina writing the words 'I love you' into the dark night sky with his searchlight. But as time passed and the young bards' outpourings grew fruitier and fruitier, the problems with this form of verse became harder to ignore. 'An egotist / in love I am', went one verse. 'Want you / to be mine / just mine / and hope never / to be nationalised'. Love poetry could be awkwardly at odds with a state that valued collective ownership over private property.

There was a question of whether the lack of formal and ideological discipline had not been just tolerated but encouraged by the circle's previous leader. Rolf-Dieter Melis, a thirty-eight-year-old Stasi officer who had been stationed with the Guards Regiment for almost two decades, had been not only the group's coordinator but its most prolific contributor, inviting the suspicion he had kept the group alive mainly as a forum for himself. Melis loved droll stories told in a rollicking iambic pentameter, and could not resist a rhyme where he saw one. At official functions, Melis wore his charcoal-black hair slicked into a neat side parting and handsomely filled his Guards Regiment's uniform. But poetry for Melis was a place where you could let it all hang out. He would rhyme *Sache* with *Sprache* even though the first word is pronounced with a short 'a' and the second long. 'This song is very popular / In our country the GDR,' went another one of his ditties. He enjoyed verses that put a smile on people's faces, even if the jokes were obvious. 'When new recruits line up in a row', Melis advised his fellow officers in his poem 'Premiere', 'Don't be too earnest and proud by half, / Don't be afraid to let them know: / This is serious business, but who doesn't like a laugh!'

Berger had tried to push the debate into a less frivolous direction. He brought along sonnets by Johannes R. Becher, Bertolt Brecht's awe-filled poem 'The Moscow Workers Take Possession of the Great Metro on 27 April 1935', and Maxim Gorky's paean to Lenin. The preponderance of Russian history in these works was no accident. East Germany's foundational myth was a negative one: its foundation was *anti*-fascism. The GDR was not West Germany, which had banned the Communist Party and thus had no one to prevent it from falling back into fascism. The heroes of the GDR's early history were street fighters of the anti-fascist resistance like Ernst Thälmann, but many of them had died before victory was in sight, executed in Nazi prisons. East Germany borrowed its political vocabulary from the Soviet Union: it had a politburo, a *centralni komitet* or Central Committee, and the Stasi had a unit for Agitation and Propaganda, or agitprop. The Soviet capital of Berger's poetry was 'eternal Moscow', 'a house that is a city [. . .] a multilingual home'. If the Stasi poetry circle wanted to write about positive origin stories, to tell narratives that involved the drama of a revolution rather than just a formal fusion of two parties, it was encouraged to turn to Russia.

But Berger's efforts had only yielded moderate results. Melis, who remained in the group as a participant, had done his best by penning a very earnest, non-rhyming poem about the Russian War Memorial at Treptower Park, called 'Gratitude to the Soviet Soldier'. Located a dozen kilometres down the road from the Guards Regiment, the monument to the five thousand Russian soldiers who died during the battle for Berlin in 1945 would have been a familiar sight to all its members. They would all have known the giant, thirteen-metre-high Red Army soldier, who stood atop a pile of broken swastikas, and the small, frightened German girl on his arm. Melis's poem tried to tell this girl's story, but it did so in emotional hues that verged on melodrama. 'Her father's joy / her mother's pride', the child had suffered the hardship of Berlin's post-war famine, 'hungry and ill / cursing the war / so recently won, / on the verge of despair'. The 'Soviet soldier from the Urals' became her saviour not just because he liberated her from Hitler's fascists, but because he 'shared his rations / for days / and more . . . / until the danger was averted'. In the penultimate stanza, the poem made a revelation to melt his readers' hearts:

That child of nineteen forty five
is now
my wife,
a happy mother.

But 'Gratitude to the Soviet Soldier' was really less a poem about the Russian army than about Melis and his claim to fame.

Among the more artistically ambitious in the circle, there was at least a willingness to engage with the ideologically overburdened formal framework that Uwe Berger handed down to them. Though more often than not, it would come crashing down on the author. Björn Vogel, a thirty-two-year-old trained cattle breeder from Naunburg whose career in the Ministry for State Security's archive department had been spurred on by his talent as an athlete but held back by a persistent stutter, read out a poem called 'Dialectics'. While not strictly a sonnet in the way East Germany's cultural founding father had envisioned it, the fifteen-liner tried to press the official philosophy of the Soviet Union into verse form. 'On a hard wooden bench / of the W50', Vogel set the scene. 'The barrel of my MP in my hand, / my steel helmet / rubbing painfully against my thigh'. That was the thesis: a soldier must watchfully defend the peace. 'Then I think / about the apartments / we could build / instead of barracks.' Antithesis: why have an army if you want peace? But Vogel's synthesis is nothing like the analytical process that Hegel, Marx or Becher imagined it to be. Instead, it's the original thesis again, an order the Chekist executes without further question: 'Then / at the shooting range / I take aim with calm / and precision.'

Another way to tell the story of the beginning of East Germany's socialist experiment would be to start with the return from exile of another writer who fled the Nazis: Friedrich Wolf. Born in 1888 in the Rhineland, Wolf embodied everything the Nazis despised: a Jew whose experience as a military surgeon on the battlefields of the First World War had turned him first into an ardent pacifist and later a card-carrying Bolshevik, his first plays made a passionate case for the legalisation of contraception and the abolition of paragraph 218 of the German criminal code, which outlawed abortions. Wolf's Second World War was more geographically fractured than Johannes R. Becher's: he had stumbled from Germany to France, France to Moscow, from Moscow back to France even though he wanted to join the International Brigades in Spain, into a French internment camp and finally back to Moscow thanks to a forged passport – all with a wife, three children and a string of lovers in tow. Like Becher, he was handed the responsibility of building up the culture sector of the new East German republic as soon as he set foot on Berlin soil in 1945, helping to establish the film studio DEFA, setting up the East German branch of PEN international, publishing an art magazine called *Kunst und Volk*, and chairing the association of East German theatres. In 1949, the GDR's President appointed Wolf ambassador to its fellow socialist state, Poland.

But if Johannes Becher was the idealistic angel sitting on East Germany's shoulder, humming sweet songs of a utopian republic built on the laws of poetry, Friedrich Wolf was the GDR's little devil, whispering a much blunter message. In a short fairy tale he wrote in 1922, a common house goose called Begbeg expresses her exasperation with her colleague, the nightingale: while Begbeg works day-in day-out to feed herself, so that she will eventually feed her master, the nightingale doesn't lift a finger and yet is adored by the farmer. 'You lazy creature, what do you do all day?' says Begbeg. Reading between the lines, it's not hard to recognise the nightingale as a symbol of the kind of poet Becher admired, and the hard-working goose as a cipher for Wolf's poetic ideal. A poet fit for the modern age, Wolf believed, needed to write 'without frills and plush', 'without sentiment, psychology . . . and ambiguity'. His tastes were so austere, he wrote in one essay, that he longed for a state in which leather became an unaffordable luxury good, so that men and women started to roam the streets of Berlin barefoot again, in touch with the soil as God intended (it is no surprise that Friedrich Wolf was one of the Weimar Republic's leading advocates of nudism). If Becher had lobbied politicians to give a special status to literature, Wolf turned around and pointed his finger at the writers. Those who really wanted to enjoy privileges in the coming socialist state had better make sure their writing played its part in furthering the socialist cause. Mere entertainment, 'luxury, caviar and opium', designed only to distract workers from the ugliness of 'the grey everyday', was not good enough. Art as a mere 'crutch' for workers' education was worse. If Prometheus wanted his rebellion against the gods to last, he needed to give the people fire. Art, Wolf believed, was a weapon – a slogan he first coined in a 1928 poem and sharpened in a speech the same year: 'The material of our age lies in front of us, hard as iron. Poets are working to forge it into a weapon. The worker has to pick up this weapon.'

Wolf's slogan was older than the idea of a socialist German republic, but it had sticking power. The East German Free Democratic Youth movement adopted the phrase as the central motto of its cultural mission and continued to organise events with the same title well into the 1980s. In September 1981, Konrad Wolf, one of Friedrich's four sons and an influential film-maker, gave a speech called 'Art is a Weapon' in front of senior officers of the National People's Army. Especially inside the Stasi's offices, Wolf's phrase was as familiar as the first verse of the GDR's national anthem – and not just because another of his sons, Markus, was the head of the foreign intelligence division, effectively the secret police's number two. In 1980, on the occasion of the 103rd anniversary of Feliks Dzerzhinsky's birth, every member of the *Wachregiment* at Adlershof was handed a pamphlet containing a panegyric Friedrich Wolf had written about the founder of the Soviet Union's secret police, the Cheka. Dzerzhinsky, he reminded the soldiers, always made sure that 'the content of literary works by Writing Chekists' could become effective as a 'weapon in the ideological class struggle with imperialism'. Becher's airy ideal of a 'literature society' was inspiring, but it was hard to tell what it really meant when you were trying to put pen to paper. The idea that poetry could be a secret weapon was more practical in comparison, especially if your entire existence was dedicated to a struggle to fend off the enemies of socialism.

At the end of one poetry meet-up in Adlershof in the summer of 1982, circle leader Berger asked the trainee soldier Alexander Ruika to read the poem he had brought along. Aged nineteen, Ruika was not only younger than most of the other Chekists in the room, he also wasn't really a proper Chekist yet: the young men who were accepted to complete three years of military service as 'Dzerzhinsky soldiers' at the Guards Regiment were not fully fledged members of the Stasi. Graduation into the GDR's secret police was not automatic for trainee Chekists, but easier than for those who only served the legally required eighteen months of military conscription. Similar to Melis, the poem Ruika had brought along was also about a monument, one he had seen when his father and grandmother had taken him on a trip to the Lviv Oblast in Ukraine when he was fourteen. For hours they had driven through the Pontic steppe with nothing but an uninterrupted line on the horizon, until their car suddenly stopped in front of Valentyn Borysenko's enormous iron sculpture. It depicted commander Semyon Budyonny's 'Red Cavalry', which had played a vital part in the Bolshevik victory in the Russian Civil War of 1918–20. Ruika's poem started with a description of bucolic harmony: the monument looked as if the ground had begun to billow 'in soft waves' towards the 'round sky', and then hardened into a 'green bow'. In the first five lines he uses a technique called enjambment – stretching the syntax of a sentence across line breaks – with the effect of slowing down the poem's flow, building an arc analogous to the one he describes. From then on, almost every second line is end-stopped, and the poem begins to move faster. Inside the green arc are the men on horseback – in the German, Ruika uses the phrase *die erznen Reiter rasen*, 'the bronze riders rearing', using a technique called consonance, stringing together words with the same consonants but different vowel sounds. The bodies of horses and riders are pressed together – he makes words jostle for space to convey a sense of movement in confinement: 'limb to limb, and pluck to pluck'. The 'soft waves' are now a 'rowdy cloud / guided by thunder'. By the second stanza, the sculpture is no longer a sculpture but a chaotic movement of real bodies, animal and human, and Ruika imagines himself to be one of Budyonny's red riders, feeling the weight of the Nagant revolver in his belt, screaming the cavalry's battle cry as they fly across the landscape. The poem is written in free verse, but there is a covert AABBCC rhyme scheme that links lines 3 and 7, lines 9 and 11, and lines 28 and 31. The effect on the listener is one of belatedly catching on to a rhythmic pattern underneath what appears at first to be chaotic movement, matching the sentiment of the poem's final lines.

As if
the land
were to flow
in soft waves
toward the round sky
and frozen
into a green bow
in the hoofbeat
in the trumpets blaring
toward the horizon
the bronze riders rearing
limb to limb,
and pluck to pluck
pressed together
as a rowdy cloud
guided by thunder.
I pull myself up
and mount.
On my belt
I can feel the Nagant
Vpered! Onwards!
In many languages
I hear this cry
that my own voice
joins in with.
My field-grey coat –
A swirl in the spume
of grey ore,
I hear the hoofbeat
As if their beat
were my heart.

When Uwe Berger finally broke the silence in the room on the first floor of the Guards Regiment in Adlershof, he said something he had never said before in their circle. All the other Stasi men would remember it for years. 'Look at this young man, comrades,' he said. 'What a talent.'

Lesson 4

METAPHOR

An expression that describes a person or object by
referring to something that is considered to have similar
characteristics to that person or object.

One reason Alexander Ruika stood out from the rest of the Stasi
poetry circle is because he seemed to understand something elemen-
tal about poetry: that writing poetically involved the art of holding
more than one idea in your head at the same time. In his *Poetics*,
Aristotle had argued that this was the cardinal virtue of any good
poem, and that the ultimate test of a poet's skill in this respect was
their use of metaphor: the device whereby a term with a literal meaning is used to convey another, non-literal meaning by association or
comparison. 'To be a master of metaphor', Aristotle wrote, was 'the
greatest thing by far': 'It is the one thing that cannot be learnt from
others; and it is also a sign of genius, since a good metaphor implies
an intuitive perception of the similarity in dissimilars.'

The poems of Alexander Ruika, published in anthologies,
newspapers and literary magazines that I managed to track
down from archives and second-hand booksellers over the following months, were full of metaphors – some intriguing, some
puzzling, some downright odd. In 'Spring Birds', published in
an anthology of young people's poetry in 1986 by Verlag Neues
Leben, Ruika describes driving down the autobahn on his motorbike one Saturday in April. As he flies over the asphalt, he sees 'a
red kite rising high above me', 'a stork crossing my path', and 'a
gaudy-feathered drake, passing through my field of vision'. As the

45

headwind punches the smell of pine forests into his lungs, the poet feels 'a kinship' with these birds. Ruika doesn't mean that he is literally related to these animals, of course, but in a metaphorical sense, there is something about the avian roaming instinct that he recognises in himself. A metaphor, the author Mardy Grothe once wrote, is 'a kind of magical changing room', where one thing momentarily becomes another and allows the reader to see that moment in a new way. In 'Spring Birds', the motorcycling poet Alexander Ruika temporarily becomes part of the natural world. Then, in an unexpected reversal in the final stanza, the natural world becomes part of Ruika and his motorbike:

> We were flying
> Until the sun
> hung red on the horizon
> like a full-face helmet

Critics pricked up their ears when Alexander Ruika read out his poems. 'Who says our technological age does not allow for original images from the poetic reserve forces?' wrote a reviewer for *Neues Deutschland* in August 1981. 'Spring Birds', the critic Hannes Würtz wrote, was emblematic of precisely the kind of emotional urgency or *Sturm und Drang* he had been missing from the new generation of East German writers. In 1981, the year before he was introduced to the Stasi circle, Ruika had presented his poem at the annual 'Poets' Seminar', a kind of training camp for the GDR's up-and-coming artistic elite, held at a romantic old castle in the north-eastern town of Schwerin. 'If the Poets' Seminar wants to survive, it needs to remember its youthfulness,' wrote Würtz. Many of those who attended the gathering in Schwerin would go on to forge impressive careers after reunification. On one of the symposium's printed programmes I found in the British Library, there were names of speakers who later won prestigious literary prizes, garnered critical praise and gained powerful roles in the arts. One had been lauded for her work by the Berlin city senate. Another was now in charge of a well-respected theatre in southern Germany. A third had gone on to win the biggest literary prize in the reunified country, the German Book Prize.

But what had become of Alexander Ruika? There were references to strings of awards that reaffirmed his early potential. His first poem was published when he was barely in his teens. Those that followed appeared in all the leading literary journals, in national newspapers and on state radio. Twice he was a runner-up in the Berlin Literature Prize and received the Free German Youth's annual incentive award. And yet, all the archives and catalogues I searched indicated that Ruika had for some reason failed to live up to his promise. There were no prize-winning anthologies of poetry to his name, no bestselling novel, not even a critically-acclaimed-but-commercially-unsuccessful collection of short stories. Instead, typing the name Alexander Ruika into Google took you to Germany's open register for limited companies, where Ruika was listed as the director of a business called B. I. S. According to its own website, B. I. S. specialised in installing security systems for private or commercial properties, but also offered 'detective services', such as 'finding missing persons', 'surveillance of employees during sickness', 'planting undercover detectives in your business', as well as digging up evidence of 'misdemeanours in relationships'. What had happened to the young man who had silenced the room with his poem about the Red Riders of Lviv?

———————

The East German state kept a detailed file on every citizen in gainful employment. The so-called 'cadre file' would chart their professional development from primary school through to their retirement home, by means of school reports, memberships of political parties or state-affiliated bodies, criminal records, payslips and workplace assessments. But in a state that believed it had overcome the bourgeois distinction between private and working life, the cadre files also cast light on life outside the workplace, via health certificates, records of holidays and trips to West Germany, reports of activities that the state security apparatus interpreted to be subversive, and detailed accounts of family members, friends and lovers, and their ideological leanings. All organs of the East German state had access to these files, including the secret police. Since January 1992, the surviving cadre files have been held by the Stasi Records Agency, which has its headquarters in Berlin and twelve further regional offices across eastern Germany. Ordinary citizens can view their own files at one of the Stasi Record Agency's reading rooms. Historians and journalists can also apply to view the cadre file of members of the Ministry for State Security, like Alexander Ruika, and its unofficial collaborators.

'We don't toe the line', starts one of the poems that Ruika brought along to the poetry seminar in Schwerin.

We watch your step
We judge, we sentence
and we pardon
We are / an INSTITUTION

The title of the poem, 'My Noble Family', is another metaphor, because Ruika did not literally come from aristocratic stock. Instead of inheriting an elevated status, he explains in the final stanza, his family had acquired theirs through hard work: 'We never had privileges / [. . .] / Never lived / off others' toil – / THAT IS OUR NOBILITY'. Ruika's Stasi cadre file only partially backs up this boast. His father was originally from Lithuania, with a surname that had been Germanised during the Third Reich. Having witnessed the terror of Nazi rule, Ruika senior had become enthused by the East German vision of building a new state and pursued a career in the military with focus and determination. Ruika's father rose to the rank of colonel in the East German army before becoming an officer at the Defence Ministry. In 1970, the Ruikas even moved to Leningrad for a year, where their son Alexander, born 30 August 1962, attended the GDR's general consulate's school. This is the part of the poem that doesn't stand up to scrutiny. The privilege that came with being a member of what the Russians call the *nomenklatura*, the holders of key positions in the Soviet Union's bureaucratic system, may not have always felt like one: back at secondary school in suburban Berlin, Ruika's cadre file notes, he was bullied by classmates because of his father's political affiliations. But if the state offers you a leg-up not available to others when you find yourself in a tight spot, then privilege is the right word: in 1974, young Alexander was transferred to another school in Berlin-Friedrichshain, 'upon recommendation of the central public prosecutor' and with the explicit permission of the Department for Education.

The full name listed in the cadre file is Alexander Os Ruika, his middle name meaning 'axis' in Russian: a nominative determinant for a young man whose poems often have an invisible tipping point – a repetition, a play on words, a contradictory image – where the meaning suddenly lurches into its opposite. In 'My Noble Family' it's in the second stanza, where Ruika suddenly writes that 'We work / to survive / but would rather / live to work.' The boosterish pride in the family line of work tips over into self-doubt: what if working for leisure is a greater achievement than fighting for survival? Was there necessarily more dignity in serving the nation than working for yourself? In Alexander Ruika's family, that alternative approach to life in the Soviet sphere was embodied by his mother, or so the cadre file suggested. The daughter of a Ukrainian mother, she had a Slavic heritage to which she drew attention by wearing long sarafan-style dresses with floral patterns and tasselled shawls, as well as writing books for children and young adults that took their readers on adventures into the unknown wilderness of the Soviet Union. Yet hers was not the Russia of Moscow central command but the remotest corners of Siberia, full of folk customs and fairy tales. Her book *In Search of the Copper Fairy* tells the story of a young boy, named not Alexander but Axel, who goes on a trip to Russia to learn about minerals and precious stones, only to lose himself in a dreamworld full of mythical creatures and enchanted lizards, after drinking a cup of tea made from taiga berries. Like her husband, Ruika's mother was a member of the Socialist Unity Party. But she believed in the existence of an inner world that had the right to shut itself off from the reach of the Central Committee.

Alexander Os Ruika's CV depicted a man who oscillated between the life of duty and the sphere of dreams. After completing a two-year apprenticeship as a printer at the publishing house that brought out his mother's books, he seemingly changed direction in 1981, following in his father's footsteps by joining the Guards Regiment on a three-year assignment. But life in the military was tough. The Erkner compound where he was last stationed was even further from the centre of Berlin than that at Adlershof. The exercises and duties he had to carry out were mundane and largely irrelevant to the functioning of the state. He was allowed to leave the site twice a week, between eight o'clock in the evening and midnight, which was barely enough time to get home and back. Only once every three months did he get a weekend off. One winter night in his second year, Ruika dislocated his knee during judo practice. His superiors were displeased when they discovered he had dragged himself out of the sports hall anyway and driven all the way to Berlin to see his girlfriend. As punishment, he was under orders to stay on his hospital bed for the next twelve weeks. In the poem 'Disagreement over Orderliness', Ruika ponders whether 'order and happiness / are mutually exclusive'. Was orderliness perhaps 'a deformation, a disease / that you succumb to in your twenties?' Ruika was torn, even more so because he also understood that discipline could have a purpose. 'What is it that troubles me? / Why do I resist?'

The Guards Regiment was not just an ordinary military unit where young men could while away their obligatory service. It was also an elite training ground from which the Stasi would frequently recruit new talent for special missions, such as the 'tunnel unit' that was tasked with preventing underground escapes to the West. But the thought of life as a full-time spy filled Ruika with horror, or so his poetry suggested. 'Every human / has a craving / for disguise,' he concedes in 'Masks'. The hunter's instinct may even be a 'habit from pre-human times'. But to him, 'pretending to be someone else' looked like 'courting behaviour / play acting'. His generation had been offered a chance to do things differently, Ruika wrote, to have the 'courage to disrobe':

Away with the masks
the world of humans no longer a hunting ground
admit you are yourself
accept yourself
and your neighbour too.

At the end of his three years' service, Ruika had more options than most, a mark of the privileged: graduates of the Guards Regiment stood a higher chance of gaining sought-after university places and could apply for generous stipends. But the Hamlet of the Stasi poetry circle was forever holding two thoughts in his head at the same time, slowly approaching one conclusion before retreating back to the other. In his head and his heart, the writer was determined to wrestle with the fighter. No poem of his articulated the questions going around his head at night better than 'Workshop or Armoury': 'Now tell me / all of you / for whom / do you write poems?' he asks, above all of himself.

Some people build cars.
Others drive them.
You write poems.
Which of the people
whose work you live off
understand them?

As a teenager, Alexander Ruika once came eighth in the national motocross championship, and his poems frequently not only featured chromed motors but also sounded like a dirt bike whose driver was frantically shifting gears to pull himself out of the mud. The final stanza of 'Workshop or Armoury' is not a synthesis but a howling motor: 'For fuck's sake, / now I want to ride my motorcycle!'

Did Ruika eventually free himself? His cadre file, frustratingly, was incomplete. Millions of pages of Stasi files were destroyed in the dying days of the GDR – burnt, shredded and torn up by hand, randomly and seemingly without a system. And in Ruika's case this meant his file was full of gaps where I was looking for answers. The Stasi Archive don't actually allow you to wander around their stacks. Instead, after you apply to view someone's file, you are assigned a case worker who compiles a file for you. When there are gaps in the cadre file, the case worker can search elsewhere for duplicates, though this takes time. In the meantime, I went back online. Company filings showed that Ruika's business had at various points been registered at three different addresses in Berlin, two in the north, one in the east of the city. One November morning in 2015, I left my apartment with three letters carrying the same message: would he talk to me about his poems and his time with the Circle of Writing Chekists? No one came to the door after I rang the bell at the first address, at the end of a footpath in Mahlsdorf. There was no movement behind the curtains when I rang the doorbell at the second, a large detached house in a leafy street in Hermsdorf. At the last address, in the suburb of Hohen Neuendorf, a young woman opened the door. It was Alexander Ruika's daughter. Her father was out, she said. I thrust my letter into her hands. Could her father call me on the number I'd included in the letter? I'm sure he would, she assured me. On the train back to my apartment, I was brimming with optimism. Days passed, then weeks, then months. Slowly, I began to accept that Alexander Ruika would probably never call me.

One question was gnawing away at me. Reading Alexander Ruika's poems, I understood why his talent had commanded so much attention in the Stasi's poetry circle. But the more poems I read by the circle's teacher, Uwe Berger, the less I understood why he sat in the room as the group's tutor, revered as an authority on matters lyrical. The English literary critic and poet William Empson believed there were two ways, broadly speaking, to account for what made a poem good. He described the first of these as the 'pure sound' school of thought: the idea that a poem turns words into music. The main argument of the 'pure sound' approach, Empson wrote, was that it identifies an extreme oddity about how poetry acts: 'the way lines seem beautiful without reason'. 'The Tyger', the William Blake poem I had read so many times with my pensioners' poetry circle in Kings Cross, was a good example of a poem whose brilliance could be explained in terms of 'pure sound'. Blake builds up a thumping rhythm with a series of poetic devices: a galloping AABB rhyme scheme, repetition (the couplet 'Tyger, Tyger, burning bright / In the forests of the night'), and assonance, the resemblance of sound of syllables of nearby words ('Dare its deadly terrors clasp?'). 'The Tyger' is a song that builds its own backing band, playing a music that can capture you even if you don't speak the language. The beat that drives the song does not necessarily have to be as merciless as Blake's. In the case of Bertolt Brecht, a poet much more popular with Berger and his East German contemporaries, the rhythm is more usually that of a ballad, and rhyme is used sparingly. 'Memory of Marie A', a poem that I forced myself to memorise in order to impress the members of my poetry circle at the Kings Cross day centre, walks with the timeless poise of a *vers commun*, a ten-syllable alexandrine with a caesura after the second foot, elegantly held together by the second and fourth, and sixth and eighth lines of every stanza. Uwe Berger's poems, by contrast, were rarely overtly musical. Early in his career, he wrote verses that rhymed, such as 'Death in Winter', from 1952:

> New snow must fall,
> The dead must rest,
> Every one of us all,
> has a past to divest.

> Things won, things lost:
> his life is now done.
> Ground hard with frost,
> A new journey begun.

But by the early 1970s, Uwe Berger's poems rarely rhymed at all. The metre was unremarkable, the repetition, assonance and onomatopoeia lacking in ambition. Berger's go-to poetic technique became the cheapest of them all: anastrophe, the Yoda method of inverting the syntax of a sentence to convey a sense of depth or drama ('of blood the earth is wet', 'of tanks is the square surrounded', 'not those who fail are great').

According to the second school of thought outlined by Empson, and one to which he very much subscribed himself, this should not necessarily matter. A line, he argued, could be highly poetic even if it lacked rhyme or metre. Instead, the 'essential fact' about poetic language was its compactness. By pressing words, ideas or statements into the restricted space of a few lines, Empson wrote, 'the reader is forced to consider their relation for himself.' This is why Empson, like Aristotle, believed metaphors to be the indispensable tool of a poet: they were 'effective from several points of view'. In 'The Tyger', Blake's metaphor is that God is like a blacksmith – 'What the hammer? what the chain? / In what furnace was thy brain?' – and a somewhat deranged blacksmith at that, forging terrifying tigers as well as innocent lambs. In 'Memory of Marie A', Brecht's metaphor is that love is like a cloud, transient yet eternally memorable for its transience.

But the Stasi circle's poet-in-chief Uwe Berger employed metaphors only reluctantly. The subjects of his poetry were poetic in the sense that they dealt with the kind of things a poet was expected to write about: descriptions of landscape, such as waves lapping on the shore of the sea, clouds meandering across the sky, fresh snow falling on frozen ground, cherry trees blossoming, birdsong, or remembrances of romantic encounters, hands touching under tables, a pre-coital embrace, a sleeping lover's steady breathing. But these were not metaphors. On the contrary, Berger seemed intent on turning the very principle of how a metaphor works on its head. In his 1970 poem 'Vapour Trail', Berger spends the first two stanzas painting a picture of an aeroplane's condensation trail cutting across the sky, 'swirling fantastically', seemingly headed for the sun on the horizon. Since the vapour trail is already the subject of the poem's title, you could be forgiven for thinking it may not just be a literal vapour trail but a metaphor, perhaps for modern technology's Icarus-like temptation of fate. But Berger quashes any such speculation with the third and fourth stanza:

What the picture
only simulates
is already reality:
Earth, sky and even
the galaxy are inhabited
by man.

'A story of particular facts', Shelley wrote in 'A Defence of Poetry', 'is as a mirror which obscures and distorts that which should be beautiful; poetry is a mirror which makes beautiful that which is distorted.' But Berger's poems were more often than not just a mirror that deprived reality of all enchantment, making the ordinary look only ordinary. A vapour trail that seems headed for the sun, his poem says, is a sign of technology's progress. The metaphor is not a metaphor but a fact.

'Does the poem serve the truth or not?' That was the central question Berger said every poet should pursue. But the truth he was pursuing in his poetry just seemed utterly mundane. The more I read of his work, the more I struggled to understand how it merited the numerous prizes and accolades he had received. Perhaps the gulf in literary taste between East and West, between pre- and post-Wall worlds, was deeper than I had thought? But when I dug in the archives for reviews Berger received at the time, it emerged that he similarly failed to inspire his contemporaries. In April 1979, the Halle-based newspaper, *Freiheit*, published an article about his collection *Quiet Words* that borders on a hatchet job, bemoaning the 'simplification of historical matter', 'images that don't work, even when you make willing allowances for poetic licence', and a lack of 'contradictions'. Sometimes writers who regularly get panned by critics inspire a particularly vociferous loyalty among their readers, but this doesn't seem to have been the case either. In May 1984 Uwe Berger wrote a letter to his editor at Aufbau, complaining that there hadn't been a new edition of *Quiet Words*. 'Specialists in the GDR and abroad', he claimed, had 'begged' him for a copy, and when he told them there weren't any reprints they were 'taken aback'. Berger was irritated to hear that the latest work by a female poet writing for a rival publishing house had been printed with a run of twelve thousand copies. He was convinced, he wrote, that a reprint with a similar run was 'not just justified but would quickly sell'. His publisher reluctantly agreed to print another three thousand copies, but added that the actual demand for the book was realistically 'more like a couple of hundred copies at most'. 'It can't be in your interest that we print a second edition we can only partially sell', the editor added, wearily.

In addition to the unremarkable quality of Uwe Berger's literary works, another feature of his poetry was puzzling. This writer, whose intellectual and moral 'inner world' had prevented him from joining the Socialist Unity Party, wrote unabashedly partisan poetry. In 1970, Berger wrote 'Song About the Border', set to music by Eberhard Schmidt, in which he hailed the 140-kilometre fortified inner German divide as a 'class barrier', a border 'between profit and our power', 'between yesterday and today', 'which protects our work, and the people who liberate themselves'. In June 1977, Berger had said in an interview with *Neues Deutschland* that to him it was 'more important [. . .] to be a politically engaged person than to make art, more important to be a Communist than an artist'. Two years later, the same newspaper published his poem 'Eastwards', which paints the Soviet Union as 'the place towards which the earth is turning', where 'wisdom prevailed', where 'man's inner world / was turned inside out / and a rising revolution / lent strength to wisdom'.

This seemed to be a remarkable position for an artist to hold: the idea that under socialism people must not have an 'inner world' at all, but wear it on their sleeve for everyone to see.

Perhaps Berger was merely playing to the censors' gallery so he could express his more conflicted thoughts in private? The archives cast doubt on that theory. On 23 September 1981, Berger spoke up at a board meeting of the East German Writers' Union, held behind closed doors. Earlier that month, Poland's independent union Solidarity – the first trade union outside state control in a Warsaw Pact country – had held its first congress and passed a programme proposing free local and regional elections and the establishment of a second house of parliament. According to archived minutes of the meeting, Berger warned that 'the counter-revolution in Poland is becoming a means of blackmailing us', and advocated a 'long-term' solution. Increasingly overwhelmed by the strains of the Soviet–Afghan war, the politburo in Moscow was reluctant to employ its military to crack down on Poland in the way it had done in Budapest in 1956 and Prague in 1968. But Berger disagreed, citing the poet Friedrich Hölderlin as inspiration: 'Where there is danger, also grows the saving power.' What Hölderlin hadn't understood, he added, was that sometimes the growing power didn't grow of its own accord but needed executive orders from above: 'Necessary steps are often recognised and taken, but then you have to actually recognise and take them.' One imagines from his comments that Berger was pleased when martial law was declared in Poland that December; some ten thousand people were rounded up and about a hundred died in the weeks that followed.

There are several ways to define poetry, many of them contradictory. But as a bare minimum, one usually expects the writer who goes to the lengths of composing a verse to have

done so because he or she has a complex inner life – intellectual or emotional – which is in need of expression. Lord Byron
called poetry 'the lava of the imagination whose eruption pre-
vents an earthquake', and one expects this boiling mass to have
a certain urgency. Yet in the case of Uwe Berger the lava inside
proved strangely elusive. At his first job after the end of the war,
as an editor at an educational publishing house, Berger was ridiculed by some colleagues as an 'aesthete' who required political
re-education: after one of the senior editors caught him talking to a visitor about poetry, he was sent down to the printers'
workshop to spend more time with manual labourers. One
young employee called on him to join the Free German Youth,
the Socialist Unity Party's official youth movement, but Berger
declined, saying he preferred to spend time in his own interior
world. 'Inside, outside – I don't understand that,' the co-worker
replied. 'If you are a decent human being, then there's no world
inside you other than the world you can see from the outside.'
In his 1987 memoirs, Berger concludes this anecdote with the
following reflection: 'I had nothing to respond to that. [. . .] In
truth, my inner self was always on his side.' But if Berger's inner
self was dressed in the Party's uniform, why didn't his outer self
show these colours too?

Lesson 5

PERSONA

*A persona, from the Latin for mask, is a character taken on
by a poet to speak in a first-person poem.*

Memoirs usually start off with a life lesson. The lesson at the start
of Uwe Berger's first memoir, *Path into Autumn*, published by
Aufbau in 1987, is that power can be seductive even when it breaks
your nose. Berger's parents had been caught between two fronts
when Hitler swept into the Reichstag in 1933. On the one hand,
his father's status as a deputy officer in a masonic lodge spelled
trouble when the Nazis banned Freemasonry in 1934, declaring
its members willing participants in a Jewish conspiracy against
Germany. On the other hand, young Uwe noticed that the fear in
his mother's eyes was just as great when communists paraded the
red flag through the streets of Emden at night. The playground,
however, provided its own political education for the banker's son:
he saw that Red brutes were often better at keeping the Nazi tide
at bay than well-behaved children from 'progressive' households.
His juvenile mind became fixated on Franz, a docker's son who
could floor the meanest school bully with a hook to the chin. 'I
admired, I loved him,' he recalled. Already playground friends
with Franz, Berger vied to become his second-in-command, and
one lunch break challenged his idol's best friend to a boxing duel.
Blows landed on his face and neck, but he swallowed his pain and
hit back until his opponent fled the ring in tears. Now that he
had proved his mettle in the street, surely his working-class hero
would look on him as an equal: at last, the son of the bourgeoisie

had redeemed himself. But Franz didn't shake his hand. Instead, he started to beat the living daylights out of the middle-class wannabe street fighter. Shocked and heartbroken, Berger let the punches rain down on him. The way Berger describes the incident in his memoirs, it is in that moment he decided to become a writer, developing a 'yearning to be different'. If the proletariat won't recognise you as one of their own, his reasoning appeared to be, you have to find a different path to power.

That alternative path opened itself up to Uwe Berger when the enforcers of the 'avant-garde of the proletariat' came knocking on his door years later. This is how he recalls the incident in a second memoir, *Outbound Paths*, published in 2005: on 1 May, 'maybe in 1970', Berger attended a book fair in a cinema in East Berlin, and overheard a group of writers talking critically about the Soviet Union. Soviet troops had invaded Prague twenty-one months earlier to intervene in Alexander Dubček's attempt to loosen restrictions on freedom of speech, press and movement. Berger decided to take a stand: 'And Auschwitz? And Treblinka? Did they not kill a lot more people there?' One of the men responded that murder was murder. Berger rebutted him: anyone who talked like that was a fascist.

The incident did not go unnoticed. A few days later, a Stasi officer in civilian clothing turned up on the doorstep of his apartment to enquire about his willingness to work as an informer. *Inoffizielle Mitarbeiter* or 'unofficial collaborators', known within the Stasi as 'scouts' or simply 'IMs' and among the general population as 'snitches', were employed in East Germany on an unprecedented scale. A total of 620,000 informers were listed on the Stasi's books between 1950 and 1989. In 1989 alone, there were 189,000 of them, meaning there was one IM for every eighty-nine East German citizens. Their role, according to the official guidelines, was to inform the Stasi about tendencies and opinions among the population, and function as an early warning system for potential threats to the state, or 'political–ideological diversion'.

Berger was not disinclined to this role, and approached the conversation with the swagger of someone with the power to negotiate a 'special status', as he recalls the episode in his memoir. He was designated an 'informal collaborator on special operations', an informant with an unusual or specialist skill or knowledge. His handler, a Stasi officer called Rolf Pönig who had little knowledge of or interest in the arts, and a penchant for calling himself *König* or 'king', gave him the imaginative cover name 'Uwe'. But the way he described it in his memoirs, Berger had staked out some red lines: he would file reports on 'problems', but would make 'no proactive approaches' with the aim of eavesdropping, and engage in 'no targeted assignments'.

———

The Stasi Records Agency informally distinguishes between 'victim files', for those who were spied upon, and 'perpetrator files', for those who did the spying. Some of the perpetrator files are slim, a few pages of standard forms at the beginning followed by a couple of loose sheets of handwritten reports. The file with the name 'Uwe' that a Stasi Records Agency archivist had placed on a reading-room desk for me one summer morning in Berlin was weightier: six volumes held in faded brick-red cardboard folders, each holding around 350 pages. A total of 2,214 sheets of A4, 432 of them written by hand. They dated back to November 1969, when the Stasi first approached Berger about a collaboration – six months earlier than the date remembered by the narrator of his memoir for his first contact with the secret police. The first meeting with Stasi handler Pönig took place on 6 March 1970, between 3 and 5 p.m., at Berger's own flat. After that, they continued at regular intervals, roughly once a month. Berger would receive 100 Ostmark as a fee for each meeting or report. Pönig's reports are often hard to read, full of words that are crossed out as the Stasi handler corrects himself mid-sentence, and with circles over the i's that make his handwriting look like that of a child. Berger's reports, by contrast, look as neatly scribed as a marriage certificate, with a straight line over every 'u' to make them easier to distinguish from an 'n' or an 'm', and the occasional word underlined for dramatic emphasis.

Berger's claim that he used his informant status to report on 'problems' wasn't an untruth: on 2 August 1973, he overheard a group of people having an argument on Alexanderplatz and ran home to call the Ministry for State Security, because he was concerned that the men who had started the argument were in fact West Germans pretending to be Easterners (the men, he told his handler, had made a 'well-kempt, bourgeois impression'). Some of what Berger perceived as 'problems' were less incidents than opinions, set views or prejudices among the wider population: the kind of information that democratic governments may have tried to obtain through surveys rather than espionage. For example, Berger reported on a conversation with a multiracial bookseller working at a shop underneath Friedrichstrasse station, who said that the most arrogant customers he had served were West Germans, and the 'friendliest, most tolerant and understanding' had been Americans. Perhaps Berger really was a patriot and had the best interests of the country at heart. Perhaps his informant activity was the direct line through which he tried to put constructive proposals to the government. If minorities in East Germany felt sympathy for the enemy, then the state should know and work out why that might be. In his memoirs, Berger recalls that in his meetings with his handler, 'I also touched upon problems that were uncomfortable for the GDR and was met with understanding.'

But when you are an informant, the line between the political and the personal can be hard to draw. The majority of Berger's reports were concerned not with broader social trends but with the behaviour of specific individuals. In some cases, this amounted to gossip. In his first written report, authored on 5 March 1970 and presented at the first meeting with Pönig the day after, Berger grassed on a writer colleague who was tipsy at an editorial meeting even though he had given up alcohol two years earlier ('he is an alcoholic'). Another report told of a respected literary figure who 'gave off the impression of being a bit senile', and a further colleague was reported to the Stasi as psychologically 'unstable'. Nothing escaped Berger's petty eye: one novelist he informed on had allowed a widow to 'stroke his cheek' at a conference – and left the building with her afterwards. Not all the gossip Uwe Berger passed on was that innocent, however. In August 1970, Berger paid a visit to the home of Paul Wiens, a colleague on the board of the Writers' Union who himself served the Stasi as the informal collaborator codenamed 'Dichter' ('Poet') from 1962 until 1982. Wiens, Berger reported, was watching West German television and made positive remarks on a news report on Marshal Josip Broz Tito, the Yugoslav leader who had defied Soviet hegemony by leaving Cominform, the official organisation of the International Communist Movement. His colleague, Berger added, also allowed his children to watch a *Tarzan* film. In another report, he described a conversation with the Jewish-German writer and journalist Jan Koplowitz, who had

told him that an institute in West Germany was working on political jokes with the intention of circulating them in the East. 'We
must not underestimate our enemy!' Koplowitz had said. This was
another one of those 'problems' that it would seem fair to inform
a government about. But a line in Berger's report is striking: 'The
question that poses itself is, why does Koplowitz know or want to
know *which* jokes are fabricated in such a manner?'

Writers don't tend to have access to state secrets, but they do
often have exclusive access to manuscripts that have been recently
published or are about to be published. On 23 April 1970, Berger
proudly reported that he had managed to get Paul Wiens to lend
him one of his as yet unpublished essays about Lenin, which he
copied out in full before handing it back. The contents, he explained
in a detailed analysis, 'did not correspond to our political views'.
Most of the time, he did not even have to employ subterfuge to
obtain manuscripts. From 1955 onwards, Berger was regularly con-
tracted by his old employer and future publishing house, Aufbau,
to review new books they were considering for publication. These
were personal critical assessments of the literary merit of a manuscript, but when the value of a piece of writing is defined by its
political content, the personal and the political can become insep-
arable. 'My concern', he wrote in a letter to Aufbau on 29 July 1971,
'is that my publishing house produces good, partisan poetry'. In
view of his lucrative activity as an informant, Berger's critiques for
Aufbau were merely a sideline, however. Genuine deep dives into
the authors' psychologies were preserved for a second report, handwritten by Berger and addressed to his Stasi handler, Pönig. It was a
remarkably efficient way to review books: Berger had direct access
to a steady supply of previously unseen manuscripts, whose merits
he assessed in a short note (a manuscript by novelist Sarah Kirsch,

for example, was quickly dismissed because it was positioned 'against socialism and the GDR'), which was then recycled within a more in-depth report for the Stasi, before he took the time to take the book apart in more detail.

A report on a short story by Günter Kunert argued that far from being merely 'an artistic failure', the work was in fact an assault against socialism itself: by suggesting parallels between socialism and fascism, the author was 'defaming in the interest of imperialist manipulation', using a method that could be 'traced back to Goebbels'. Kunert revealed a 'nihilistic, cynical, duplicitous attitude that without doubt takes on a counter-revolutionary quality'. Monika Maron's manuscript *Josefa* also 'showed counter-revolutionary tendencies' and 'talked down everyday life in the GDR'. Behind an anthology by the poet Uwe Kolbe, Berger detected the 'guiding hand of imperialist diversion headquarters', the seeming hurly-burly of words amounting to a 'counter-revolutionary programme'. The writer Franz Fühmann had a 'fascistoid fondness for intoxication and magic'. Through the surreal verses of poet Lutz Rathenow, readers were 'emotionally, animalistically, psychopathically prepared for suicide and murder': this poetry was nothing less than 'political manipulation', reminiscent of 'Hitler fascism'. Closet fascism was one of the favourite accusations Berger would level against his fellow authors – a somewhat self-contradictory assertion, given that he would almost in the same breath denounce other writers to the Stasi for making 'the absurd accusation that we have fascists over here'.

Uwe Berger's reports were more powerful than the iron fists of his childhood idol, Franz the docker's son. He could punish enemies, sideline rivals and build up allies, all with the stroke of a pen. His meetings with Pönig became little seminars with an attentive audience of one, in which he would expound on his views on literary theory and global affairs: when West German Chancellor Helmut Schmidt met with East German leader Erich Honecker in Güstrow in December 1981, Berger explained the historic significance of the meeting in a detailed IM report.

The way the informant on a special mission wrote his reports gradually began to change. Berger made a habit of referring to himself in the third person, as if he were writing small dramas with himself as the protagonist: 'Uwe Berger said', 'Uwe Berger rejected this', 'he conceded a point to Uwe Berger'. Uwe Berger became an institution, an organ of state, and by that logic any attack on Uwe Berger also became an assault on the legitimacy of the GDR. In July 1975, he submitted a note to the Stasi in which he complained about recent criticism of his poems from both East German authors and West German journalists: a review in the left-leaning *Frankfurter Rundschau* had dismissed his latest anthology as too solemnly lofty. Berger smelled a conspiracy, 'a coordinated approach' by Western capitalists and Eastern dissidents. When the editor of *Neue Deutsche Literatur* expressed reservations about publishing one of Berger's articles, he complained to the Stasi: 'Berger's defamation reveals a common method, whereby the Party is attacked via an attack on someone without Party membership, who is thought to be unprotected.' The man whose conscience had apparently once prevented him from joining the Socialist Unity Party was now thinking of himself as a loyal bodyguard, taking hits to protect the Party's honour.

An informant with a 'special status', who reported only on 'problems' but would not make 'proactive approaches' or take on 'targeted assignments': if that was really once the agreement between Berger and the Stasi, it did not survive for long. Within a few years of taking up his role, Berger was no longer content with merely supplying information: he began to suggest how his information should be used. Sometimes he advised against acting upon the information supplied. In September 1972, he told Pönig about a tragic mix-up he had heard about at Köpenick hospital, where a patient had suffered serious internal injuries after mistakenly receiving an enema of hydrochloric acid. Going public with this story contained risks, Berger warned, because it could be 'used by the enemies of our health system'. In a report on the work of the poet Thomas Erwin, he attested 'a certain proximity to Social Democrat demagoguery', but advised against a concerted campaign of intimidation: the 'artistic value' of Erwin's poems was simply too low for him to have a lasting effect on the public.

But in other reports Berger endorsed the Stasi using his information to crack down with full force. 'The IM is of the opinion', Pönig wrote after a meeting on 28 January 1972, 'that the GDR should no longer put up with effrontery and provocations': the best solution would be to deport offensive writers to West Germany, not least because it would have an intimidating effect on others. By the end of the 1970s, Berger's reports to the Stasi were full of calls to arms, packed with military jargon and the metaphors his poetry lacked: critical authors were 'oppositional gangs' who 'strive for hegemony' in order to carry out 'frontal assaults'. Before innocents got caught in the 'crossfire', he advised the Stasi to further 'scout out territory' before eventually 'pushing [them] against the wall'. A 1979 collection of poems and lyrics by the singer-songwriter Bettina Wegner had drawn his ire for 'creating and gradually increasing a general feeling of unease, of disappointment, disgruntlement' that could potentially turn into 'emotional tinder' for appeals from the 'other side'. The eager informant suggested 'primarily

psychological means' of unsettling the target, such as getting
left-leaning journalists in West Germany to criticise her songs.
If Wegner's popularity in East Germany were nonetheless to
increase, Berger recommended the coinage and circulation of a
catchy put-down. His humble proposal: 'tampon poetry'.

In February 1982, the Stasi rewarded Uwe Berger for his enthusiastic and reliable contributions by handing him the silver
'Brotherhood in Arms' medal, a military honour that the
Ministry for State Security would only occasionally grant to
individuals outside the armed forces. After two officers had
handed the eager informant the white cloth ribbon with two
orange stripes, Berger expressed his gratitude and reiterated his
willingness to work for the secret police again in the future, or so
a report of the meeting claims. 'He described himself as a patriot
without a Party affiliation, who was on the side of the working
class and its Party.'

Uwe Berger does not mention the medal, or the contents of any
of his reports, in the post-Wall volume of his memoirs. The book
makes his collaboration with the secret police sound like a tire-
some chore, without any real consequences, and at any rate rather
short-lived. 'A couple of years' after starting to write reports,
Berger recalls, he asked his handler to release him from his commitment. As an artist, he reasoned, he could not be constantly
exposed to the 'negative aspects of life'. At a secret location, over
dry bread rolls, two senior officers granted him his wish. There
was only one condition. In return, Uwe Berger was asked to take
over the artistic direction of the Circle of Writing Chekists at the

Guards Regiment. Seven years earlier, he had snitched on two writers who had suggested that circles for writing workers mainly produced 'verses about boozing, vomiting and shitting'. Now he had the chance to prove them wrong, so he agreed. From reading Berger's memoirs, you would assume that his appointment as poet-in-chief at Adlershof in 1982 was when his career as a spy came to an end.

Lesson 6

BATHOS

*An effect of anticlimax created by an unintentional lapse of
mood from the sublime to the trivial or ridiculous.*

For Stasi staff, life inside the institution was one of exotic adventures outweighing small personal sacrifices. East Germany's 'scouts for peace' travelled from Siberia to Bonn under forged papers to infiltrate the West German government. They swooped into South America to expose former Wehrmacht officers plotting a resurgence of fascism. They dashed arms deals in Portugal, retrieved chemical weapons from shipwrecks at the bottom of Norwegian fjords, muffled war drums in Turkey, prevented CIA coups in Greece and spoiled plans to inject the entire West German army with a drug known as 'King Kong Flu' that would induce aggressive behaviour. The lack of family life could be tough, but it all became more bearable when you had to bed busty blonde neo-Nazis to avoid blowing your cover along the way.

That, at least, is how the life of the Stasi's elite force was portrayed in a series called *Das unsichtbare Visier*, which first aired on East German television the day before Christmas Eve, 1973. It was not only the opening sequence of this series that was modelled on the adventures of a certain British super-spy who regularly featured on West German TV: at the start of each episode, a suited figure appeared in the middle of a blue-tinted circle to the sound of a stalking bass line, pausing before turning to the camera at the cue of a wailing horn section. East Germany's James Bond was called Werner Bredebusch. Played by the dashing young Armin Müller-Stahl, he was intended by his creators to embody 'a socialist scout excelling in partisanship, steadfastness, bravery in battle, self-discipline, readiness to make sacrifices, cleverness, [and] creativity', and he did so with great swagger.

But the reality of serving the Ministry for State Security did not always match up to Bredebusch's adventures on the East German small screen. The number of Stasi employees dedicated to foreign, as opposed to domestic affairs, dwarfed those working for James Bond's employers: by 1989, there were nine to ten thousand full-timers at the Ministry's reconnaissance branch, compared to 2,300 officially recorded as employed by MI6. But foreign affairs for the Stasi mostly meant West Germany rather than derring-do in exotic locations, and in the vast majority of cases their work consisted of paper-pushing. The growing number of informal collaborators came with a growing number of handwritten reports or minutes of secret meetings, and the volume of paperwork produced in the process needed to be kept in order. Björn Vogel, the second-oldest member of the Stasi poetry circle, had entered the Ministry in 1970 and joined the archive department, which collated and organised information gathered by its wide network of full-time and informal spies. His poem 'Night Shift' tries, and struggles, to imbue a daily routine of data processing with the glamour of a life of ejector seats and exploding pens:

Between night and morning
A radio call
Quickly!
Frenzy.
Phones ringing, teletypewriters chattering.
Tired yawns, but excited concentration.

Precise research through
Accurately filed matter.
Information
To the comrades.
Quiet pride –
Mission completed
In the struggle for peace.

———————

The Stasi had always thought of itself as more than just an ordinary secret police force. When the GDR's first President, Wilhelm Pieck, had appealed to Josef Stalin in 1948 for his fledgling republic to have its own spying agency, his pitch rested on the proposal that the Stasi would be modelled as closely as possible on the Soviet Union's legendary 'All-Russian Extraordinary Commission', the Cheka. Even in the 1980s, employees of East Germany's Ministry for State Security still referred to themselves as 'Chekists', and the internal room-booking sheet at Adlershof described the monthly meet-up not, say, as the 'Stasi poetry club' but as the *Kreisarbeitsgemeinschaft Schreibende Tschekisten*, the 'Working Circle of Writing Chekists'. In Russia, the Cheka had presented itself as a state security organ of a new type: as the historian Julie Fedor writes in her book on the mythologies of Soviet state security, the Cheka's foundation 'marked the dawning of an entirely new era in the state policing of society'. It was distinct from the Tsarist guards, the Okhrana, with its own moral code and a spiritual aura. Chekists, the Russian writer Isaac Babel wrote, were 'sacred people', whose mission was to bring to the enemies of the Revolution 'a spiritual bath in death', in poet Velimir Khlebnikov's phrase; Lenin hailed them as 'proletarian

Jacobins'. These were supermen of subterfuge, who were required to achieve nothing less than a seemingly impossible equilibrium of intellect and passion: a burning dedication to their moral cause, an emotional detachment from the human sacrifices required to achieve it, and an utter immunity to temptations of the flesh and lucre. A brass plate, fixed to the wall at the bottom of the staircase one floor down from where the Stasi poetry circle met, regularly reminded its members of these high ideals. Engraved underneath a stark portrait of 'Iron Feliks' Dzerzhinsky, whose hollow cheeks lent him more than a passing resemblance to depictions of Jesus, were three criteria for what made a good spy: 'Only someone with a cool head, a hot heart and clean hands can become a Chekist.'

The Chekist mission statement contained some contradictions not apparent at first sight. These elite operatives had to prioritise their professional lives over their family commitments at all times: their work must never be discussed with parents, partners or children. But at the same time they had to be utterly truthful to their employers. They had to be hard and unyielding, but also completely transparent in their actions – which is to say they must never be able to turn their hardness against the Party that controlled them. The second line on the commemorative plaque at Adlershof found the right metaphor to gloss over this seeming paradox: 'A Chekist has to be more clean and honest than anybody else,' it read. 'He has to be as clear as a crystal.' The image of the crystal was central to the original Cheka's mythology: in a 1957 poem that dramatises the moment Lenin selects Feliks Dzerzhinsky as the man to take charge of suppressing counter-revolutionary activity, Soviet writer Semen Sorin imagined the anointing to have been accompanied by 'glass tinkling from a nearby explosion / As though the ice of the Neva was breaking'.

One of Russia's biggest manufacturers of technical glass is still named after the Bolshevik spymaster, as is Dzerzhinsk in Nizhny Novgorod Oblast, east of Moscow, a town famous for the production of crystal and glass. One defining characteristic of crystal, as East German students of crystallography knew, is that it is inherently symmetrical, made up of identical repeating patterns.

The older members of the Stasi poetry circle in particular had uniformly committed themselves to this hierarchy of values. Björn Vogel, born in Saxony in 1949, had joined the Stasi as a twenty-one-year-old under difficult circumstances, with his recruiters forcing him to break off an engagement before they allowed him to join the ranks: his former fiancée's stepfather was a 'returner', an escapee from East to West who had later changed his mind and thus remained a potential risk factor. Once Vogel had signed up, his professional progress was slow, impeded by a physical disability and family matters. His stutter came to the fore every time he had to operate under stress, and speaking in front of large groups or to strangers was difficult for him. In March 1982, his name was crossed off the personnel reserve list of young officers who had the potential to move up to a higher official role. Earlier in the year the Stasi had thrown out his younger brother, who had been employed for three years in the same department, once it was discovered that he was gay. Homosexuality had been decriminalised in the East five years earlier than in the West, but the Stasi had its own moral code, which meant gay members of its force were potential targets for blackmail and therefore an unwanted liability.

All these personal slights and sacrifices, in addition to the evidently mind-numbing mundanity of his everyday work routine, had made me think Björn Vogel might be open to a conversation about his past. He was easily found on social media, and his profiles were public. From LinkedIn I could glean that he used to work as a caretaker, but the pictures on his Facebook profile gave the impression that he was deep into retirement: photos of the beach in his home town of Kühlungsborn, glasses of craft beer in restaurants, Vogel bobbing in the Baltic Sea in Świnoujście, grinning. In the digital sphere, he was a willing sharer of likes and dislikes: I discovered that he kept fit in old age, using a walking app that automatically posted updates onto his timeline. I learnt that he was still sceptical of American politics, posting articles about US-led wars from the Russian state-sponsored network Russia Today, but also a lover of American music who liked Roy Orbison, Bruce Springsteen and Frank Zappa. I learnt that he had flipped from left to right: there were clips from September 2017 that described Germany's nascent Alternative für Deutschland party as 'totally gaga', but he changed his tack after the right-wing populist party entered the national parliament for the first time two weeks later, now commenting with 'He's got a point . . .' on a video of an AfD politician condemning the US intervention in the Syrian civil war. In June 2018, he shared a video that claimed mass immigration from Africa was 'organised by powerful people like George Soros', the Jewish-born Hungarian-American financier, and that international Jewish finance networks were deliberately bankrupting African countries 'in order to subsume them into the New World Order'.

But as transparent as Björn Vogel was about his political views now, he remained secretive about his past. When I sent him a message on Facebook, asking if he would talk to me about the Working Circle of Writing Chekists, his answer was prompt and curt: 'What's that meant to be good for??' I sent several follow-ups. He never responded again. 'Strong and impenetrable /

are the walls that surround us', Vogel had once written in a poem called 'Vow'. 'It is impregnable / our fortress / because on us, comrades / you can rely'.

Keeping the Chekist flame alive was a daily struggle. No one knew this more than the man in uniform who had led the group before Uwe Berger had been drafted in. Ever since Rolf-Dieter Melis had joined the Guards Regiment as a twenty-year-old in 1964, there had been questions about his commitment to the Stasi cause. During political debates, one report noted, Melis was often cautious and reserved: 'He only takes an active role when he is asked to make a statement.' Rather than being as 'hot' as required, Melis's heart, his superiors worried, was only beating at room temperature. His hands were clean, but mainly in the sense that they hadn't seen much action: ten years into his service at Adlershof, when Melis asked his superiors for a promotion, they realised he had only acquired 'a minimum in military capabilities', skipping officer school, the section leader course and training for chief guards. Instead, Melis had thrown himself into every cultural activity available to him: he had joined a choir, a cabaret group and a folk dance class, and had taken over the organisation of the Stasi's radio studio and set up the poetry group.

But Rolf-Dieter Melis got away with these deficiencies because his ability to meet the third of the Cheka's requirements, keeping a cool head, had never seemed in doubt. Melis's cadre file records how he and his family attended the sixtieth birthday party of his father-in-law in the spring of 1975. When the couple arrived, a small group of visitors was already present. After a few minutes, Melis noticed that two people spoke in a 'foreign dialect': they were relatives of his mother-in-law, visiting from Bavaria in West

Germany. Melis immediately left the building, on the pretext of taking his daughter to a walk. The next day, according to a report he volunteered for his Stasi superiors, he had informed his parents-in-law in 'unmistakable terms' that contact with citizens from an 'NSW' or *Nichtsozialistisches Wirtschaftsgebiet*, a non-socialist economic zone, could not be reconciled with his service in the armed units of the Ministry. When he realised that his in-laws did not respect his position with the 'necessary level of understanding', he broke off all relations with them. The almost-encounter at the birthday party, during which no words were exchanged, merited a four-page report from Melis.

When I asked Jürgen Polinske whether he had stayed in touch with any of the members of the group after the fall of the Wall, he shook his head. Everyone had their own issues to deal with, he said, but artists were always a bit more sensitive, and in times of change artistic sensitivity could be a negative. Was he talking about anyone in the group in particular, I asked. Rolf-Dieter Melis, he said, had been one of the sensitive ones. After that meeting I found the name of Hilde Melis, Rolf-Dieter's wife, in the phonebook, and when I called she picked up almost immediately. But when I mentioned that I was interested in her husband and his work at the Stasi poetry circle, she said she would hang up the phone. Yet she continued talking: she and her husband had never talked about what he did at the Stasi, she said. Work always came first, then family. What about that poem her husband had written about her, 'Gratitude to the Soviet Soldier', recalling that she was the little girl in the giant sculpture at Treptower Park? Surely that must have meant something to her? There was a silence at the other end of the line. Still, Hilde Melis did not hang up. Instead, she offered a prime example of *Berliner*

Schnauze, the capital's famously coarse-but-hearty way with words: *Die hatten doch was an der Bommel*, 'Those guys needed to have their head checked.' The girl in the Soviet War Memorial, she said, had never been her. Still, Hilde Melis continued talking. After the fall of the Wall, a friend had talked Rolf-Dieter into building himself a house: getting a building permit and the necessary materials was meant to be easier in the new reunited Germany than in the old encrusted Soviet system. Melis had taken out a small loan for 60,000 Deutsche Mark to buy a plot of land in Königs Wusterhausen, south-west of Berlin, and in 1993 the building work had begun. But then the building contractors he employed went bankrupt. The family breadwinner couldn't get any more work, and Hilde was bringing in most of the cash. He couldn't get a foothold, she said, and that's why he did what he did in 1994. Before the house was finished, Melis had taken his own life. If her late husband walked through the door now, his widow said, she would slap his face. Without the organisation that had once structured his life, Rolf-Dieter had told his wife before his suicide, she was the stronger out of the two of them, and he could no longer go on. Rolf-Dieter Melis had been a good crystal until his very last day, which is to say he was transparent to the Stasi but opaque to everyone else.

One of the poems that Rolf-Dieter Melis wrote while in the poetry circle is called 'My Daddy'. It has two verses, the first of which is about his life in the Stasi:

He does not beat about the bush
always likes to give it straight:
We make changes as a team
and never moan about our fate

The second is about his family:

> My father is a Chekist.
> It is hard to see through
> everything he does when he is there
> but rely on him I do.

Most crystals aren't actually clear at all, but cloudy. Calcite is one example: a beautiful, transparent crystal in its purest form. But in the natural world most calcite crystals aren't pure. When calcite comes into contact with a gas or metal, the structure changes and the light is refracted differently. Add a bit of cobalt, and the calcite turns pink. Add some iron, and the crystal turns yellowish brown. Zinc makes the crystal go whiteish grey, and manganite lends it a mysterious violet hue. Sometimes you can make a calcite crystal clear again, but that involves exposing it to a lot of strong sunlight. If you want to keep a crystal transparent, you need to keep it in an artificial environment, isolated from the natural world.

The first generation of Stasi recruits had a crystal-like uniformity when it came to their social background. The organisation's original leadership consisted almost exclusively of long-standing members of the German Communist Party, many of whom had personal experience of underground warfare. In order to build up a secret police force in their own image, they started by recruiting predominantly those from underprivileged, proletarian backgrounds. The Ministry for State Security's head, Erich Mielke, a woodworker's son who had joined the Communist Party's paramilitary wing in his twenties, explained at a Party conference in 1953 why the Ministry actively sought out uneducated, illiterate recruits for the new and growing secret police. 'What matters', Mielke said, 'is that these comrades, who may not know how to write, know how to achieve victory and what to do in order to destroy their enemies. Let's have a closer look at all those who can write so brilliantly and give such wonderful speeches, and let's check: how many enemies have they destroyed?' The working-class background of new recruits, and their presumed hatred of the bourgeoisie, continued to be an important factor for the recruitment of new Stasi employees as socialist East Germany and its security apparatus began to grow. 'Social background: worker' is a phrase that pops up with numerous variations in the Ministry personnel files: 'The candidate comes from a working-class family', or 'The candidate comes from a family of loyal servants to the Party of the working class.' Rolf-Dieter Melis had originally trained as a locksmith and welder. Björn Vogel had completed an apprenticeship as a cattle breeder before his recruitment. Polinske, who had been to university, nonetheless came from 'a working-class household', as his cadre file noted.

But in the 1970s a growth spurt made it harder to stick to Mielke's original guidelines. While other secret police agencies in the Soviet bloc, such as Poland's Bezpieka, peaked in size in the mid-1950s, the Stasi continued to expand at a monstrous rate. The overall population of East Germany shrank over the forty years of its existence, from 18.79 million in 1949 to 16.43 million in 1989, but the numbers employed by the Ministry for State Security continued to go up. The Stasi had 20,000 employees in 1961, when the Wall was built, and more than doubled in size in just a decade, to 45,000 by 1971. Over the next ten years, the East German secret police would grow even faster, almost doubling its numbers yet again, to 81,500 employees in 1982. Owing to the high demand for new recruits, many of the Chekists from this generation who ended up in the poetry circle were defined as 'working-class' only through rhetorical sleight-of-hand. The cadre file of Gerd Knauer, a young officer in the Stasi's agitation and propaganda department who had been part of the group since 1978, insists that he came from a 'working-class family', and that 'his father trained to become a locksmith.' But by the time Knauer had joined the Ministry in 1972, his locksmith father was in fact a high-ranking lieutenant at the Stasi's training facility in Eiche, while his wife's father was a GDR diplomat who was regularly sent to advise fellow socialist states in South Yemen and Ethiopia. And then there was young Alexander Ruika, who had trained as a printer but whose father's officer status meant he very much came from what East Germans called *Roter Adel*, 'red nobility'. His cadre file struggled to find an appropriate euphemism to mask the obvious inherited privilege: 'The candidate comes from a progressive family loyal to the Party of the working class,' it says.

Poetry could help to polish cloudy crystals until they shone again: that was the idea set out for the Stasi poetry circle, to instil in its participants the hot heart that had fired up the first generation of German Chekists. An appeal from when the group was first set up in the 1960s called upon all members of the Ministry to submit poems, short stories, song lyrics or short anecdotes that gave expression to their 'love of the homeland, optimism and joie de vivre, as well as friendship with the Soviet Union'. Above all, the appeal concluded however, the rationale behind these creative writing exercises was to 'intensify the hatred of the enemies of peace and socialism'. But had that worked? By the time Uwe Berger took over the management of the lyrical task force, its recruits were writing poems that ended in questions rather than answers. 'It is within my power / to see / or to see through' went the first three lines of Alexander Ruika's poem 'In My Power': a kind of catechism laying down the skills required of the ideal Chekist. The next four lines could be read in two different ways, however: 'to integrate / or to subordinate / to evade/ or to stand my ground'. A description of the pliancy expected of a good clandestine subversive, who blends into enemy territory until the time has come to drop the mask? Or a reflection on the illusions of power bequeathed by military hierarchies, arriving at the thought that true authority may not lie in a badge on your uniform but the ability to refuse an order. The second stanza was even more ambiguous

I have been empowered
to delegate power
That has to take me into account.
This makes me mighty

In the original German, the alliteration at the end sounds naive, perhaps deliberately so: *macht mich mächtig*. A childish display of chest-beating that seems to make a mockery of the contorted self-importance that precedes it. Ruika read out another short poem in the group on the same theme, a two-liner called 'Seeking power' that arrives at the same conclusion more elegantly. 'I seek a power', it went, 'Power over myself'.

When a secret surveillance organisation looks to swell its ranks, it must also invest more energy into spying upon itself. Anyone who had followed the adventures of the East German James Bond closely would have been aware of this paradox. Plans for a Soviet counterpart to the fictitious MI6 agent had circulated in the Ministry for State Security as early as the mid-1960s, but were not acted upon at the time, which is hardly surprising in view of the broader historical context. In the first twenty years of its existence, the stability of socialist Germany had been visibly put to the test by the uprising of 1953, the construction of the Berlin Wall in 1961 and the Prague Spring of 1968. The view that the Stasi was the 'shield and sword of the Party', required to protect a fledging proletarian state from counter-revolutionary tendencies, did not require reinforcement. By 1973, however, when Gerd Knauer had joined the Stasi's Department for Agitation, the threat from which the secret police was meant to protect East Germans had become harder to define. West German Chancellor Willy Brandt's *Ostpolitik* of normalising relations with the East was in full swing: the previous year, the two states had for the first time since the end of the war signed a treaty in which they recognised each other as sovereign states. It allowed West Germans to visit relatives in the East several times a year and even made it possible for East Germans to cross the border for urgent family matters. On 11 December 1973, weeks before *The Invisible Visor* first graced East German television screens, West Germany took a further step towards diplomatic recognition of the Eastern Bloc with the Treaty of Prague, through which it recognised Czechoslovakia. The Bond franchise would nod towards the détente four years later with a love match between Bond and his Soviet counterpart Anya Amasova in 1977's *The Spy Who Loved Me*: the real enemies were no longer Russians, but Russians who had defected to Spectre, a clandestine quasi-capitalist operation.

The Stasi would have been familiar with the ideological trajectory of 007's adventures: in his new job Gerd Knauer noticed that a group of senior officers regularly disappeared into a basement at their offices on Berlin's Gross-Berliner Damm, where the Stasi kept a vast archive of banned Western films that had been confiscated, ranging from soap operas to porn films and spy thrillers.

The East German James Bond, however, was conceived as a reminder of the need for watchful spies, justifying the expansion of the secret police as relations between East and West seemed to thaw. In the pilot for the new TV series, French soldiers complained that their American and British allies had done too little to rid the West German government of Nazi sympathisers: exiled Luftwaffe officers were plotting to seize power in Bonn, and talk of a 'United States of Europe' was in fact a front for West German imperialism. In later episodes, Stasi agents battled NATO plans to provoke military escalation with the GDR, uncovered a secret weapons programme in South Africa, and revealed CIA plans to stoke 'national fascist' revolutions in Greece, Turkey and Italy.

The show's title paid tribute to the old Chekist legend: the German word *Visier* carries the meaning of the 'crosshair' sights on a gun as well as 'visor'. The invisible target in Werner Bredebusch's mind mimicked the superhuman X-ray vision of 'Iron Feliks', keeping track of the enemy's movements, whereas the morally inferior James Bond was distracted by women and cars. But by episode four the crosshair sights had fogged up, and the storyline was entangled in a complicated, at times barely penetrable game of deception and counter-deception: Bredebusch, the Stasi spy who had infiltrated the West German intelligence services, is sent to Portugal to investigate the mysterious mid-air explosion of a passenger plane carrying a senior official in the West German Defence Ministry. The double agent, who has taken on a third identity as a private insurance detective, ends up at Lisbon's ethnographic museum, in a room adorned with ritual masks from the Congo, Bali and the Americas. During a tour of the displays, Bredebusch notices one of the masks staring back at him. The next day, he sets out to find who was watching from behind the mask: a shady American arms firm called Interarms, competing with West Germany to sell arms to help Portugal in its dirty colonial wars. But in order to meet the firm's director face to face, the triple-cover agent has to put on a fourth, literal disguise: during the meeting, Bredebusch is made to wear a death mask with no holes for eyes, while Interarms director Professor Godiva sits in a darkened corner of the room, her face also hidden behind a veil. It is a scene that feels symptomatic of a broader malaise: instead of dramatising the Stasi's worldly flair, *The Invisible Crosshair* laid bare a strange inwardness that had befallen its ranks.

By the 1980s, the Stasi's inwardness had intensified to the point of paranoia. At a Party conference in April 1981, State Security Minister Erich Mielke articulated his agency's world-view in terms that sounded more like a philosophical treatise than a policy directive. The existential question that every Stasi spy had to ask themselves on a daily basis, Mielke argued, was 'who is who?' – like a socialist version of the well-known British society directory. In order to answer this question, every citizen had to be watched, examined and eventually placed in one of four categories. Category one were enemies of the state, with a 'hostile-negative' attitude to the ruling Party. Category two were those who could become enemies of the state if subjected to 'hostile-negative' influence. Category three were those with 'wavering positions' in relation to the ruling Party, who were prone to being seized on and used by the enemy. Category four were those the state could trust and rely on. Mielke did not hide the fact that only a minority of East Germans fell into category four. Indeed, he conceded that a high proportion of Socialist Unity Party members and the Stasi itself were more likely to fall into categories one, two or three. Everything and everyone was a potential enemy-in-the-making and had to be surveilled. Who is who? Finding an answer, Mielke prophesied, meant preserving world peace and securing the future of socialism. For a brief moment, the head of the secret police seemed to channel Hamlet: 'who is who', he said, was a matter of being or not being.

The Stasi's institutionalised paranoia had already given birth to a number of control mechanisms. In Berlin, staff were housed in self-contained districts, which were managed by an internal administrative unit. Stasi officers played football in Stasi clubs and were looked after in Stasi hospitals when they were ill or injured, their children went to Stasi nurseries or Stasi schools: a privilege, but also a sign of the lengths to which the state was going in order to maintain complete control. Special spies, so-called UMAs or 'unknown collaborators', were secretly trained to keep a close covert watch on family members of Stasi employees. The officers themselves were made to share offices, so that comrade would always keep an eye on comrade. But what about the moment they left their desks? The Stasi needed someone to watch the watchers when they let their guards down. But it had to find a method to take the temperature of their emotions when they were dreaming, to gaze into their hearts to identify any desires that could grow into a temptation, to X-ray their souls for deviant fears and aspirations. It had a job for Uwe Berger.

The idea that a poem is always a direct expression of the poet's truest inner self goes back to the Romantic era: 'the spontaneous overflow of powerful feelings', as William Wordsworth described poetry in the preface to his and Samuel Taylor Coleridge's *Lyrical Ballads*. The notion that a poem lays bare its author's authentic inner self in a way that ordinary language cannot survived into the twentieth century, and was championed in an influential essay by the poet M. L. Rosenthal, called 'Poetry as Confession'. The best kind of poem, in Rosenthal's view, establishes an intimacy between the reader and the author, a level of trust and unguardedness that allows us to gaze deep into the poet's soul: 'The use of poetry for the most naked kind of confession grows apace in our day', is a line Rosenthal wrote two decades before the Stasi poetry circle gathered at the Adlershof barracks, but one that would have appealed even to the high-culture sceptics in the Ministry for State Security.

Uwe Berger resumed his activity as an unofficial collaborator in October 1982 with a series of short profiles that put the clarity of his young crystals under the microscope. One twenty-year-old corporal was 'sluggish', 'clumsy', with a 'low level of education', but also 'open and direct', and therefore useful: he naively confessed that other comrades had warned him off joining the poetry circle because he would be forced 'to wave the red flag' there. Another recruit, aged only nineteen, 'a lean and sensitive boy', displayed a decidedly un-Chekist 'propensity to parrot'. Some of the aspiring poets had a disconcerting habit of disguising rather than revealing their true feelings in their works. One sergeant-major, though 'undoubtedly talented', was worryingly 'cool, sceptical, self-controlled'. 'The thing to get to the bottom of', Berger wrote in his report, 'would be to find out what is really behind the mask, at the bottom of his soul.'

Most of the reports in Berger's file from 1982 onwards relate to the Chekist bards in the Adlershof circle, though there are also references from September 1983 onwards to his new editor at his publishing house. Sigrid Töpelmann, who had joined Aufbau in 1982 as the first female deputy editorial director, was a former literary theorist who had become frustrated with academia. A lecture in which she called for the state to judge writers on merit rather than against the static grid of Marxist literary theory had resulted in disciplinary proceedings against her, and a demotion to teaching at a secondary school. Unlike her predecessors at Aufbau, she was unenthusiastic about Uwe Berger's literary output, especially his manuscript for a novel titled *The Tendency*: a tale set in Belarus about a young Wehrmacht officer who joins the Russian partisan forces. 'With all due respect, and without wanting to sound too grand', she wrote to a colleague on 27 July 1982, 'you can't get away with this stuff any more.' When she wrote directly to Berger to tell him that his division of the world into good Soviets and bad Nazis struck her as anachronistic, he replied angrily: her 'sudden arrogance and intolerance' was uncalled for when dealing with a 'not inexperienced and not unknown author' like himself. He would remain wedded to socialist realism and not allow himself to be pressed into a 'contemporary literary mold'. The mission of poetry as he saw it, Berger explained, was to describe not just what is the case, but what is possible. A report to the Stasi followed soon after. *The Tendency* was published in 1984.

The subject of the largest number of reports Uwe Berger produced on any single member of the poetry circle was Alexander Ruika. He praised the teenager's galloping verses about the red riders of Lviv, as he had done in person: he called it 'a good poem'. But on paper Berger was more interested in Ruika the person: the young man had a 'conflicted character', his demeanour was 'morose, reserved and melancholy'. His poems, he added in a report in April 1983, were 'ambivalent': he had a problem with 'power' under socialism. On subjects like collectivism, life in the army and revolution, Berger reported, the young lyricist was hard to pin down: he was 'openly in favour', but 'subliminally against'. A poem called 'Dreams', Berger noted with great concern, came in two parts, one called 'Nightmare', the other 'Daydream'. In the first, the poetic voice was that of a pessimist who had lost faith in utopias: 'I know, the dreams are over'. The second half of the poem was more optimistic, if vaguely so: only by doing something could 'my dreams be kept alive'.

Berger's reports about Alexander Ruika were different from those he used to write about his own literary rivals. There are passages that speak of genuine admiration: this was a talent, he wrote, who had the means of elevated poetic language 'almost effortlessly' at his disposal. Berger wasn't entirely convinced that the nineteen-year-old had the correct political conviction to use these means 'responsibly'. But there were moments of promise. During a meeting of the circle on 30 March 1983, Ruika told the other members of the group that he had attended another literary circle of poets and novelists outside the Stasi. He recounted that at his first and only visit to this other circle, he had read out a partisan poem to a reception of rolling eyes and criticism of the East German military.

For once, Ruika had opened up to his fellow Stasi poets: these kind of people, he said, 'needed to be dealt with'. Berger took note. 'In his demeanour, Ruika is cautious, sometimes somewhat elegiac and gloomy, but he seems to love extraordinary situations in which he can prove his worth.' Berger's reports on Ruika don't read like warnings on yet another citizen the Stasi needed to keep tabs on. They read like studies of someone of whom he thought the Stasi could make good use.

Lesson 7

CONCRETE POETRY

*Poetry in which the meaning or effect is conveyed partly or
wholly by visual means, using patterns of words or letters
and other typographical devices.*

They started the engine as soon as the target left the seafood restaurant and walked across the cobbled Marienplatz. The woman had long, straight brown hair with a centre parting and a single strand of hair falling down her forehead. One of her front teeth was missing, and she wore oversized half-tinted glasses, a black coat and black flares: a tiny grey figure in a tiny grey town. Zwickau was where East Germany built its own automobile, the Trabant: a coal-burning, industrial town where the river ran as black as spilt ink and smog turned the whitest blouse grey. But the officer approaching on foot from the other end of the square had a clear view of the woman as she made her way through a crowd of lunchtime foot traffic. She had her fists dug into her pockets, her back as straight as a board. The officer stepped into the woman's path just as the car with the other four men came to a halt in front of her. 'Your presence is required,' he said, while his colleagues began piling her into the back seat, 'in order to clarify the circumstances of an investigation.' She did not put up much of a fight. One Stasi report states the time of arrest as 2.17 on a Monday afternoon, though that cannot have been as clinically accurate as it sounds: a report by another agent specified the time as 1.05. Stasi agents liked to sound like scientists, but even those without poetic ambitions dabbled in creative writing on the job.

For the Stasi's men, the swoop was the culmination of a two-week surveillance operation. They had been taking turns watching the twenty-three-year-old woman from six in the morning until seven at night. They had followed her daily commute to the local Protestant church, where, on paper, she was only employed to shovel coal: they knew that in fact she spent most days working with teenagers in the attached youth club. They had followed her to her apartment on Karl-Marx-Strasse, number 50, and watched her from a window in the flat opposite. When the professional spies came to the end of their shifts and went home to have dinner with their wives, they handed over the task of surveillance to the unofficial collaborators. Frau Tröger, a widow in her eighties with an apartment on the same floor, reported that the target was receiving several male visitors at 8 p.m. 'Party with sexual content. Probably three-way intercourse. 8:15 p.m.: calm inside the premises.' On 11 February 1980, the Stasi followed their target to a nearby town, Karl-Marx-Stadt, where she attended a poetry workshop at the Pablo Neruda cultural centre before returning to Zwickau for lunch at Banquet of the Sea, a state-run chain of restaurants serving everything from Bulgarian fish stews to fillet of herring with mayonnaise salad. Then they made their arrest.

Once the target was locked away inside a cell, they raided her apartment. A key obtained by the Department for Criminal Proceedings opened the main door. Inside the first room, a surprise: the Stasi agents awakened two teenage girls the target had met at the church youth club, sleeping on a sofa and a mattress. The terrified girls were arrested and later charged with public nuisance. Above the sofa the Stasi found a poster with the word *Angst* in capital letters. They opened the door to room number two, containing the suspect's own unmade bed next to a writing desk. Above the desk they found a poster for a Dixieland music festival in Dresden, a list of acquaintances to whom the tenant owed money, and a post-card with a picture of a witch. Then, at long last, on the desk next to a West German praline box, they eventually found what they had been looking for. They seized the offending objects, switched off the water, electricity and gas, threw out the food from the kitchen, and sealed the front door. As the Stasi squadron walked away from the premises, they carried in their arms a total of 108 pieces of paper: notebooks, folders and loose pages. One of the items was an A5 Hermes notebook with the name of its owner on the outside front page: Annegret Gollin. The inside page carried an epigraph: 'Thoughts and poems that I want to show only to friends whom I hope are true, and in whom I do not expect to be disappointed'.

———————

The more time I spent immersing myself in the world of East Germany's secret police at the Stasi archive's reading room, the more I realised that in order to truly understand what went on inside the minds of the spies, I needed to understand those who were spied upon. To make sense of the Stasi's poetry circle, I also had to find out about ordinary poets, outside the fortified walls of the Adlershof compound. Some, though not many, had become familiar names after the fall of the Wall, even to West German teenagers like me: Christa Wolf, Monika Maron, Ulrich Plenzdorf, and especially Wolf Biermann, the dissident singer-songwriter who was expatriated from the GDR due to his tour in the West in 1976. But none of these writers intrigued me as much as Annegret Gollin, whose story was mentioned in an academic paper I had picked up: a poet who was arrested and then sentenced to prison on the basis of a single poem that was never published. Two years after her arrest and seven years before the fall of the Wall, Gollin had been one of 1,491 political prisoners the East German regime sold to the West for a payment of around 40,000 Deutsche Mark, and I found out that she was now working as a tour guide at the German Chancellery, the offices of Angela Merkel. On a sunny May day in 2017 we met at a cafe near her work, swatting wasps from our lemonades.

On paper, Annegret Gollin was the kind of person East Germany's 'literature society' was supposed to have been built for. Born in 1956 in a working-class household in Neubrandenburg, the daughter of a blacksmith and a farm worker, she had developed an appetite for books by the age of five. At eleven, she decided that her favourite book was *Faust* – a choice that put her in line with Walter Ulbricht, the GDR's second head of state, who thought that Johann Wolfgang von Goethe's classic drama of struggle between progress and tradition was as important for the future of the country as *The Communist Manifesto*. Gollin began to write seriously while she was still at school, but her creative drive seemed to display an alarming lack of self-control. Other students thought long and hard before they put pen to paper – Gollin wrote constantly and everywhere, in lessons and during lunch breaks, at home, in the cafeteria, on the bus to school. Her poems didn't rhyme and had no shape. 'Why do you try to pack so many images into your poems?' a German literature teacher asked her one day. 'Why not?' the teenager replied. She wrote poems that were as crammed full of ideas as essays, and essays that were as cryptic as poems. Her homework, a school report complained, was impossible to grade. And she asked strange questions: if the Russians are our friends, why don't they go to the same school as us? Why do they all live in barracks in Neustrelitz, where we can't talk to them? Why did her school teach that Marxism–Leninism was supposed to be at the heart of all scientific knowledge, but forbade her from reading *Das Kapital?* Sometimes she laughed out loud in the middle of a lesson. 'The sun rises in the East,' said her textbook. 'But how can the sun be a communist?' Gollin giggled. Her teacher didn't answer her questions, but wrote a note to her parents instead. At home, little Annegret's impertinence earned her a smack around the face. Aged seventeen, she left school without the recommendation needed for further education. If writing books wasn't an option, she could at least work with them, Gollin thought, and she started training as a bookseller at a vocational college in Leipzig. But working as a bookseller was sobering. The shelves were brimming with works by Becher, Marx and Lenin, but all customers really wanted to read were books about cooking and gardening. A literary black market flourished under the counter: customers traded fresh sets of bed-sheets for new children's books, a bunch of bananas for a comic.

The Stasi's initial interest in Annegret Gollin wasn't triggered by her poetry. Literature had to go beyond the literary, Johannes R. Becher had said. 'Free people on free soil' was the line from *Faust* that Ulbricht had championed as the founding credo of the GDR. When she was eighteen months old, Gollin had climbed on her tricycle and cycled off through the front door, down the garden path and out into the world until her parents had to call the police. Even then, she had *Fernweh*, a longing for faraway places. And when she wasn't allowed to explore these far-flung worlds as a writer when she got older, she continued to try to find them with her feet. During her apprenticeship, aged barely eighteen, she started hitch-hiking up and down East Germany: a largely symbolic act of rebellion, because the country was small, public transport was cheap, and motorways were few and far between. But as symbols went, hitch-hiking was a powerful one. As a hitch-hiker, or 'tramper', Annegret Gollin was part of one of four growing youth movements treated with suspicion by the organs of state security and deemed to be 'negative decadent'. At the time, the other three groups under surveillance were leather-clad 'heavies', 'skinheads' in olive-green American bomber jackets, and 'punkers', whose haircuts were inspired by those of a Native American tribe the Stasi thought were not called Iroquois but 'Hoquis'. (A 1985 diagram expanded the classification of suspicious youth movements to include 'Teds', 'Poppers', Goths and New Romantics.) In the Stasi's eyes, trampers or 'bluesers' were the 'classic' style of decadent 1970s teenager. They wore washed-out jeans, parka jackets, 'Jesus sandals' and long hair. They boarded trains without valid tickets and locked the compartments behind them with home-made keys. They crammed up to six trampers a time into tiny Trabant cars, and followed 'beat music' bands touring village fetes around the socialist republic.

'As a rule,' the Stasi noted, trampers were 'not aggressive or violent', but in the case of Annegret Gollin – who was both female and unemployed of her own free will – they nonetheless merited close attention. Women were more present in East Germany's labour market than across the border in the West, and career and family were not necessarily seen as incompatible. The state encouraged mothers to return to work as soon as possible after childbirth: nurseries for children were open from 6 a.m. until 6 p.m. and paid for by the state. The moral and legal hurdles for getting a divorce were lower than in the West too: the GDR did not think of itself as a state in which the church should interfere in the life of its workers. But when it came to young women and what they were allowed to do with their free time, the GDR's moral compass was petit bourgeois. One of the first Stasi reports on Annegret Gollin describes her as 'easy', because she liked to smoke, drink, and 'approach young men in discotheques'. Her attitude to employment was also baffling to the authorities: Gollin wrote letters to bookshops in Berlin, asking if they could employ her, rather than waiting to be assigned a workplace by the state. And sometimes it appeared that she wasn't keen on working at all. The East German state took pride in being able to guarantee full employment for every citizen: unlike in West Germany, where a fluctuating market economy constantly changed the demand for labour, East German citizens had a legal right to employment. The flipside was that a refusal to work counted as 'asocial behaviour' and was rendered illegal by paragraph 249 of the GDR's criminal code, punishable by up to two years in prison. Gollin and her fellow hitch-hikers had developed a range of strategies to evade the law. Some broke their little finger with a broom handle to get themselves signed off work, while others swallowed the silver foil from a pack of cigarettes and told their doctor they had a stomach ulcer. Some cut their fingers and put a drop of blood in their urine sample.

But the workers' paradise of East Germany had a vindictive streak in its dealings with drop-outs. On 26 March 1975, a letter was sent by the Ministry for State Security's Neubrandenburg branch, declaring that nineteen-year-old Annegret Gollin was not to take up a position as a librarian at Jena University, as previously planned. Instead, it instructed the head librarian to deny her employment by creating a 'legend'– a Stasi term for a 'believable cover' that must not be traceable to the state apparatus. The applicant was duly informed that the position was already filled. Five months later Gollin was arrested for 'anti-social behaviour' at a music festival.

In a Prenzlau prison, two officers made her an offer: she could spend the next two years in a prison cell, or she could sign up as an unofficial informant, and reduce her prison sentence to six months. The prospect of jumping the queue for a new flat, and future employment in the Culture Ministry, were thrown in for good measure. Gollin agreed, but barely lasted a year before she decided to blow her own cover. The job in the Culture Ministry didn't materialise – instead, she found herself sorting punch cards in a data processing centre. By August 1976, she had told over a hundred of her friends and acquaintances of her supposed spying activity, rendering her worthless as an informant. On her twentieth birthday on 11 December 1976, she invited forty-five of her tramper friends from across East Germany to Berlin. With her savings, she bought ten bottles of wine, six crates of beer and 100 Ostmarks' worth of cigarettes, and announced at the end of the evening that she was retiring from the hitch-hiking scene. In the space of two years, she had managed to burn her bridges with both the state authorities and its counterculture. Freedom was something she could find neither in the rigid structures of Party membership and full-time employment, or among those who pursued free movement and free love. In January 2018, I met Annegret at a hospital in Potsdam, where she was being treated for a knee injury. East Germany, she told me then, was a country 'in which you could fuck everyone and trust no one'.

After her farewell party to the tramper scene, Gollin was no longer a member of a 'negative decadent' youth movement, and she should by rights have dropped off the state's radar. But the Stasi was a hungry spider. Once someone had brushed against its web, it could not let them go. It wanted to examine its catch in ever more exacting detail. And if the victim was about to extricate herself, a special kind of adhesive was required to pull her further into the web's centre. And literature was the kind of glue the Stasi had been looking for. After leaving behind her tramper friends and moving to Zwickau, Gollin joined two writing circles – one in Karl-Marx-Stadt, one in Neubrandenburg – which she attended almost every week. In the summer of 1979, Gollin's membership of these groups led to her being invited to a state-sponsored gathering of young wannabe writers in Schwerin – the same annual event that would two years later be attended by Alexander Ruika. (Unlike the young Chekist, Gollin was sent home early: she had refused to wear the blue blouse of the Free German Youth for official events.) But the poetry circles regularly attended by Gollin served a similar function to the set-up inside the Stasi: honey traps that allowed the state to attract creative or critical minds and observe them up close.

The Stasi found these groups were most effective when run by people who made their students feel sheltered from the more obviously policed world outside: caring, sensitive men and women, substitute father or mother figures. Once the budding writers let their guard down, they were encouraged to open up about their literary tastes – information then passed straight on to the Stasi. Gollin's mentor in Karl-Marx-Stadt, a quiet, seemingly sensitive woman handicapped by a club foot, offered the young aspiring writer a hand-typed copy of poems by Reiner Kunze, an East German poet who had relocated to the west after being blacklisted for his support of the Prague Spring. When Gollin then told her tutor that she could also get hold of photocopies by another dissident writer, the informant codenamed 'Sylvia' immediately passed the information on to her handler. By then, however, the Stasi had already amassed material that gave them a window into Annegret Gollin's inner life. On 22 October 1979, a senior employee at the Neubrandenburg water board, registered as a Stasi informant with the codename 'Christel', contacted his handler with an A5 booklet full of poems he had found in his teenage daughter's bedroom. In the opinion of 'Christel', and he made sure to add that he was by no means an expert on literature, these poems were directed 'against our state'. When he confronted his daughter about the notebook's contents, he claimed, she insisted that the poems were years old, and had been given to her by a former schoolfriend. When pressed for the schoolfriend's name, the daughter would only release the young woman's nickname, 'Uschi' – paying tribute to her resemblance to jazz singer Uschi Brüning. 'Uschi', the daughter said, had written the poems in a spirit of 'youthful foolishness' and had since started a new life in Zwickau. The intelligence was limited, but enough for the Stasi weavers. A few weeks later, on 6 December a copy of one of the poems from the notebook, entitled 'Concretia', landed on the desk of a Stasi informant codenamed 'Klaus Richter', who ran the poetry circle in Neubrandenburg and was a remarkably similar figure to Gollin's course leader at the poetry circle in Karl-Marx-Stadt: a frail man with a penchant for receiving visitors while a raven perched on his shoulder – a character straight out of a fairy tale. Could he identify the author of these 'negative and inflammatory verses', his handlers asked him. 'Klaus Richter' said he had read the poem for the first time approximately one year ago, when a female person aged twenty to twenty-five, wearing large metal-rimmed glasses, had consulted him for his opinion on her work. Had he heard the name Annegret Gollin before? Yes, 'Klaus Richter' replied, the female person who had shown him the poem had introduced herself by that name. In the first week of 1980, the Ministry for State Security set up a new operation, codenamed 'Transit', that culminated in her dramatic arrest and the seizure of her poems a month later.

Annegret Gollin was a non-conformist, and in the eyes of the Stasi a youthful troublemaker they wanted to constrain. Her incarceration was almost inevitable, and she could equally well have been prosecuted for smuggling cigarettes or for possession of a banned book. However, the verses for which the Stasi arrested her appeared to disturb the secret police far more than her wayward lifestyle. In the months following her arrest on 11 February 1980, Gollin was interviewed thirty-six times about her modest poetic output. Again and again the twenty-three-year-old was marched to an interrogation room and asked to interpret and explain her own poems. The police could see what her poems said, but what did they mean? Was this poem a criticism of the National People's Army? Did this line mock the Socialist Unity Party? Was this title a reference to the police crackdown on the 1977 protests at Berlin's Alexanderplatz? Every air pocket of ambiguity had to be beaten out of the pieces of paper the spies had retrieved from Gollin's flat. One of the poems, she eventually explained, was a criticism of how the East German government handled the expulsion of the dissident songwriter Wolf Biermann: 'In my poem,' Gollin told her interrogators, 'I make the claim that there is no freedom in the GDR, and that everyone who takes a political view that runs counter to that of the Party and government is being imprisoned or expelled from the GDR.' Even after the author had been made to trample over her literary work until it was flattened into a literal message, the Stasi could not quite fathom what they were dealing with. The charges against Gollin bring to mind a terrorist building home-made explosives, not a teenage girl jotting down her insecurities in her bedroom: 'In 1977, she made the decision to practice subversive agitation in written form.

To achieve this aim, she made use of certain expertise she had acquired in a literature club in Neubrandenburg, and manufactured eleven inflammatory pamphlets in verse form. These were trans-ferred from Post-it notes in her A5 format so-called literature book and circulated in early 1979.'

How could a state be so scared of a few lines of verse? These weren't poems written by a powerful, influential author admired by millions, but an unemployed twenty-one-year-old with no publishing contract to her name. They weren't photocopied verses going viral behind closed doors, but lines handwritten into a school notebook, shared with no more than five close friends. Her poem titled *Betonien*, or 'Concretia', was laid out in an unusual style, like two tower blocks of text.

I live	in the 20th century.
I live	the modern way.
I live	a super life.
I live	progressively.
I am a creature	of Concretia.
I find it	nice and interesting.
I find it	good and comfortable.
I look	out of the window.
I see	concrete to my left.
I see	concrete to my right.
I feel	good
I notice	
I think	concrete.
I become	concrete.

(That's not just the case in New York City.)

At its 1971 party conference, the Socialist Unity Party had passed a proposal for a vastly ambitious construction programme with the aim of completely eradicating housing shortages by the year 1990. Eighty-seven thousand new residential units were built within the first year alone – by 1978, a year after Annegret Gollin wrote 'Concretia', the millionth new apartment was ceremonially handed over to the Grosskopf family in Berlin's Marzahn district. Most were *Plattenbauten*, constructed with slabs of pre-cast concrete, many of them dropped incongruously onto the outskirts of small rural towns. A teenage Annegret had seen prefab tower blocks sprout like autumn mushrooms covering the hillside where she had gone sledging as a child, and had taken an instinctive dislike to them. She called them *Sachsenschliessfächer*, 'Saxon deposit boxes' – a reference to the compulsory resettlement programmes of the 1950s and 1960s, when the East German state had removed thousands of citizens from near the border with West Germany. Centuries-old regional feuds ran deep through the population of East Germany, and in the minds of Mecklenburgers like Annegret Gollin, Saxons tended to be slavishly loyal to the regime (Saxons, of course, believed the same to be true of those who lived in the north). To her, the concrete high-rises of 'Concretia' were nothing but devices to instil discipline among the population and water down the concentration of dissidents: those who live in concrete end up thinking like concrete, the poem suggests in its penultimate line. But were the Stasi really able to unpack a poem like that?

Perhaps what made Annegret Gollin's fifteen lines of verse so threatening was not what they said, but the fact that it is unclear whether they said anything at all. In his testimony to his Stasi handlers, informant 'Klaus Richter' claimed he remembered the poem so well because he had disagreed with the last line and asked her to change it. When grilled by the Stasi later, Gollin herself remembered their discussion differently: in her recollection, it was her tutor who had encouraged her to add that last line to narrow down the ambiguity. The final line, 'That's not just the case in New York City', creates another layer of meaning: uniform, heavily set architecture is a metaphor for uniform, heavily set thinking not just in the class enemy's capital of capitalism, but also elsewhere, though the poet doesn't say where. But it is a line that also removes ambiguity: without it, most people would have read it as a poem about East Germany, while being able to pretend that it's a poem about America. 'The process of getting to understand a poet', wrote William Empson, 'is precisely that of constructing his poems in one's mind.'

———————

'Just because you're paranoid', Joseph Heller wrote in *Catch 22*, 'doesn't mean they aren't after you.' And there was some evidence that authorities in the East were particularly aware of the subversive power of poetry because their counterparts in the West were too. The first post-war German Writers' Congress in early October 1947 – the gathering where Johannes R. Becher had announced that literature in the East would have the standing of a *Grossmacht* or 'sovereign great power' – had been rudely interrupted by an American visitor with a neatly trimmed beard who protested that no writer could ever enjoy freedom in a Soviet empire where aesthetic taste was decreed by the politburo. The speech drew a variety of impassioned responses from the assembled literati. Some responded with frantic applause, others with heckles of 'A foreign guest should not be allowed to speak like that!' One attendant merely shouted the name of composer Hanns Eisler: the Austrian who composed the piece of music that would become the GDR national anthem had been one of the first to be blacklisted in Hollywood during the McCarthy-era witch hunts, and had only a few months previously been interrogated by the House Committee on Un-American Activities, a group that included a young Richard Nixon.

For the interruptor, US author Melvin J. Lasky, it was the start of a stellar career in the divided ex-capital of Germany, earning him a reputation as the man who would drag America into the cultural Cold War. Bronx-born Lasky believed that in order to win the dormant conflict between the two great powers, America could not just rely on its popular culture, 'cheese-cake and leg-art', to win the hearts of the masses, but also needed to appeal to the minds of the intellectual class. Within the next three years, he was given not just one but two vehicles with which to achieve this goal. In 1948, Lasky was made editor of the West Berlin-based literary magazine *Der Monat* ('The Month'), which specialised in publishing a high-profile roster of writers and thinkers who had once been or were still associated with the political left: George Orwell, Arthur Koestler, Jean-Paul Sartre, Albert Camus, Hannah Arendt, even the Frankfurt School Marxist Theodor Adorno. And in January 1950, Lasky managed to convince the West Berlin mayor Ernst Reuter to back a broader cultural initiative aimed at gathering liberal but anti-communist writers from across the 'free world': the Congress for Cultural Freedom, which would help set up literary magazines with a liberal-left slant everywhere from France to Japan, Nigeria to Lebanon. West Berlin's efforts in the culture war would later get its own architectural monument just a few hundred metres from the Reichstag and the border between East and West: a congress centre with an audaciously curved roof, later known as the House of World Cultures. Nicknamed the 'pregnant oyster', the building was intended by its backers as a deliberate counter-statement to the showcase of new socialist architecture on Stalinallee boulevard on the other side of town – in the words of the new congress centre's champion, Eleanor Dulles, sister of the CIA director Allen Dulles, it would be 'a bright beacon shining light into the east'. By the time the world came to be gripped by the arms race, the arts race was already in full swing.

If the East had openly declared art a weapon, America had been more covert. In 1966, the *New York Times* revealed in a series of articles that the CIA had been secretly transferring funds to false-front organisations – a year later, it emerged that the Congress for Cultural Freedom had been one of them, and that American intelligence agencies had more or less directly funded the careers of leading intellectuals, artists, musicians and writers across the Western world, including Jackson Pollock, Stephen Spender and even one of the towering moral authorities of the West German literary world, Heinrich Böll. In East Germany, this was barely news. It merely confirmed what authorities and the press had said from the beginning. As early as June 1950, Johannes R. Becher had declined to appear on a panel organised by Lasky with the words 'I don't debate with snitches', and East German newspaper *Neues Deutschland* had published an open letter that exposed what it called 'the biggest culture scandal of the century': 'It is a fact that this Congress [for Cultural Freedom] takes place under the protectorate of the American secret service.'

By the start of the 1980s, however, the idea that American spies were still actively trying to worm their way into East German writers' minds through literature seemed increasingly far-fetched. The Congress for Cultural Freedom had closed down in the wake of the *New York Times* scandal, and though East German newspapers still occasionally asked correspondents to dig up dirt on its successor organisation, the International Association for Cultural Freedom, they usually returned empty-handed. *Der Monat* shut up shop in 1971 and Lasky headed to London to edit its British counterpart, *Encounter*; an attempt to revive *Der Monat* in 1978 proved short-lived and lacked the influence of its original incarnation.

And yet the Stasi kept on searching for camouflaged infiltrators. The fact that they weren't able to unmask more spooks did not convince them that the Americans were less active. On the contrary: surely it had to mean the class enemy was using ever more sophisticated means of disguise. In 1979, graduates of the Ministry for State Security's own academic institutions in Potsdam took a closer look at the 'counter-revolutionary events' of Budapest 1956 and Prague 1968, and came to the conclusion that cultural actors were particularly vulnerable to Western influence and could easily be turned into capitalism's 'ideological multipliers': 'If external enemy powers manage to mislead persons from this field, to bring them under their influence and eventually build them up into a fulcrum of enemy support, then this offers them a variety of opportunities to realise their subversive plans to create an inner opposition inside the GDR and other countries.' The screws on the once so privileged literary class had already been tightened in the wake of protests against the state's treatment of expatriated singer-songwriter Wolf Biermann in 1976. Any author who wanted to be published had to first submit their book to the Culture Ministry, where it was thoroughly frisked for subversive content. The Ministry did not use the word 'censorship', but described this process as 'appraisal'. Outright bans were indeed rare: because the state had sole control over the supply of paper, it could easily pressure publishers to withdraw works, seemingly of their own accord. Surveillance work was scaled up: operation 'Transit' against Annegret Gollin was one of roughly a hundred and fifty formal proceedings against writers that the Stasi set up between 1970 and 1989. In July 1979, Culture Minister Hans-Joachim Hoffmann visited the Stasi headquarters on Normannenstrasse to focus the snoops' minds on the threat posed by poets, 'these people with whom we have for the last three years been living in an open feud.' 'Linie XX/7', the state security department dealing with cultural activity, was boosted at the start of the 1980s, growing to around 170 full-time employees.

Deep down, perhaps the Stasi didn't really believe Western spy agencies were using poems and novels to covertly undermine East German morale. Instead, there seemed to be something integral to what poets did that they perceived to be subverting the state. The authority of the Socialist Unity Party, a party that was 're-elected' every three to five years in a non-free, non-secret vote, rested not in the mandate of the electorate but in the claim, inscribed in the country's constitution, that only the Party was able to read Marx, Engels and Lenin in the correct way. Intellectuals who came up with alternative readings were an instant threat. The case of singer-songwriter Biermann is well known, while that of Rudolf Bahro less so: three years before Annegret Gollin's arrest, the philosopher was arrested on trumped-up charges following the publication of *The Alternative*, a treatise arguing that the East German government had failed to overcome the capitalist division of labour diagnosed by Marx and therefore remained only a proto-socialist state. The Bahro saga, which ended with the socialist intellectual migrating to West Germany in 1979, was symptomatic of a philosophical battle between the state and its internal critics over words and what they were allowed to mean.

One mechanism through which the Socialist Unity Party sought to control the use of language was the publication of a lexicon, first printed in 1967 and then updated every three to five years: the *Little Political Dictionary*. The dictionary defined the Berlin Wall not as a barrier for people who wanted to leave the country but as an 'anti-fascist protection wall': the Wall, it explained, had 'secured peace' by spoiling Western plans for a military conflict, and put a stop to the 'plundering' of the GDR by the West German republic. The dictionary's definition for the word 'opposition' was that such a concept could not exist in a socialist state: in bourgeois political systems, parliaments were divided between parties in and out of government. In East Germany, however, there was 'no objective social or political basis for an opposition' because the working class was both the ruling class and the main source of economic productivity. The entry for the word 'freedom' involved a similar degree of contortion. 'Freedom', it claimed, citing Engels, was not the 'imagined independence from natural laws . . . but the recognition of these laws'. Because all 'material and spiritual un-freedoms' had already been overcome under socialism and communism, the *Little Political Dictionary* concluded, workers in the GDR already lived in the 'realm of freedom'.

No paycheck from a Western spy agency was required for poets to brush up against these linguistic constraints: in Annegret Gollin's case, she ran into conflict with the official definition of 'freedom' upon her arrest. In spite of its twenty-four-hour surveillance operation, the Stasi had missed something about the twenty-three-year-old until the arrest on 11 February 1980: she was three months pregnant. In September the previous year, Gollin had married Harald Schlieder, a tall and lean hitch-hiker with long hair. On 28 March, the court case against the nega-tive-decadent poet was put on hold for fourteen months to allow her to give birth and begin to raise her child. When the court verdict came through in 1981, it was more lenient than expected: Gollin was ordered to hand over her poetic oeuvre and take up regular employment, and given only a suspended sentence of two years. She could enjoy her freedom within the limits set by the state. But Annegret Gollin decided to put her freedom to the test: on 7 March 1982, she asked a friend to babysit her son and met a group of friends at a dance hall in Ebersbrunn, for her first outing since becoming a mother. Alcohol was cheap, and her friends were generous. By 6 p.m., she had had nine shots of Mocca Edel schnapps. As she walked from the dance hall into the bar area, a friend pointed out a young man with curly hair, whom she recognised from her hitch-hiking days. Her group had regarded the young man as a suspicious character: he had told some people that he had studied philosophy, others that he had studied medicine, and generally seemed a bit too eager to make friends. Gollin went up to the man and laughed in his face: 'Don't think you can make friends just because you're wearing a disguise,' she said. 'We still don't want to have anything to do with you.' In the ensuing scenes, the man pulled Gollin's jumper. 'I know what you think,' he said, according to Gollin's later testi-mony in front of the police. 'Yes, I am with the Stasi! It's my job to get you into prison and your child into state care, so that it is brought up properly.' Gollin called the man a pig and spat in his face. He spoke up, so that everyone could hear him: 'Have a look at this woman: she smokes, she boozes, and she has a child at home. And she claims to be a mother!'

On 19 March, Annegret Gollin was sentenced to twenty months at a prison in Karl-Marx-Stadt: one year reactivated from her previously suspended conviction and eight months for 'public vilification of an organ of the state'. Her son was sent to a children's home. In December, she found out that her son's father had died, supposedly of an accidental gas leak at his home, though the circumstances were suspicious: her late husband had trained as a gas-fitter and lived in a flat with a persistent draught. One of the poems for which Gollin was sentenced to prison was called 'I Laugh at You', containing the following lines of blank verse:

Shut your gob, you shouted
And threw a punch
Now I am missing my front teeth
And I call out twice as loud
for freedom.

One of the books Annegret Gollin had discovered during her apprenticeship as a bookseller conjured a vivid picture of the East German state's relationship with language. Notionally a children's book with language games, poet Franz Fühmann's *The Steaming Necks of the Horses in the Tower of Babel* centres on a group of friends whom a Turkish ghost called Küslübürtün teaches about palindromes, anagrams and rhyme schemes, as well as introducing them to the ideas of Arthur Schopenhauer and Karl Marx. The central metaphor of the book, and Fühmann's central metaphor for the state of the GDR in the late 1970s, was the biblical Tower of Babel: a structure, as his child students are quick to point out, that could not have been built without a common language. How else could its architect have conveyed to the builders what he had in mind? But having a common language made the workers too powerful: they would have kept on building the tower until it reached into Heaven. In the Book of Genesis, God decides to confuse the people's common language, and scatters different tongues all over the globe. Fühmann, an idiosyncratic Marxist, read the Old Testament myth against the grain: the confusion of language, as he saw it, was not a punishment from on high, but a feature of the division of labour, something he regarded as an inevitability rather than a bourgeois aberration: 'It started with the division into hunting and farming, which literally divided the tribes – farmers were stuck in one place, but the hunters roamed the land.' Farmers needed to find new words to distinguish types of plant, while the hunters were content to stick with 'grass'. 'Work has created language, but work has also confused language,' says the little green ghost in baggy salvar trousers. Fühmann's book is a celebration of the anarchic mess of language, its inconsistency and absurd beauty. The most ridiculous character in *The Steaming Necks of the Horses in the Tower of Babel* is the officious librarian Herr Leipzig, who speaks in the jargon of the Socialist Unity Party and warns children off 'nonsense' poems that 'don't convey progressive knowledge or useful feelings'. 'Sometimes I like poems because they are beautiful and nothing else,' the children reply. 'Is that so bad?'

Fühmann's book passed the censors, but the message between its lines was slyly subversive. One way to read it was as a kind of DIY manual for encrypting and decoding the confused language of a confused regime, a manifesto for poetic terrorists like

Annegret Gollin or the poet Uwe Kolbe. In 1981, Kolbe's sixty-two-line poem, 'Core of my Novel', ended up on the desks of the Culture Ministry's censors. The state-sponsored assessors were used to scrutinising texts for diversion tactics, obviously provocative so-called 'white elephants' or 'porcelain dogs', designed to distract them from the more subtle criticism the writer really wanted to get across. But Kolbe's poem raised no suspicions and got the all-clear. Only after publication did state officials realise they had failed to read the poem the right way around: if you strung together the first letter of each word in the epic poem, you got the following message:

Your measures are miserable
Your demands enough for bootlickers
Your formerly blood-red flag blows
Into a sluggish belly
To the victims of your heroism I dedicate
An orgasm
May you mighty old men be torn apart
By the daily revolution

Since some writers had been able to evade their censors in such a humiliating fashion, the Stasi concluded it needed to get even better at understanding the machinations of poetry. In April 1980, the Ministry for State Security's own think tank, the Chair for Scientific Communism, produced a thirty-page position paper on 'solutions to problems in the field of cultural politics and its current political and political-operative consequences'. Quoting Lenin, it reminded the Chekists that 'a war can be won in a few months, but in the field of culture it is impossible to achieve victory in such a short time'. The cultural Cold War required greater tenacity, more patience, and more systematic planning. Especially at a point in time in which 'real existing socialism' seemed to be winning on the economic, political, and military front, it argued, the threat on the culture front was greater than ever before. A good Chekist had not just to train himself physically, but to sharpen his eye when it came to detecting forms of literary subversion. Art and culture, the Stasi think tank concluded, were especially prone to 'covert and subliminal assaults', because their practitioners employed unusual ways of reflecting on the 'objective reality' of the real world, among others 'allegories, metaphors, fables, alienation effects'. To disarm these new enemies, the secret police needed a young Chekist who had access to their arsenal and understood how it worked.

Lesson 8

HEROIC POETRY

*Narrative verse that is elevated in mood and uses a
dignified, dramatic and formal style to describe the deeds of
aristocratic warriors and rulers.*

The Stasi had developed an interest in Alexander Ruika's connections to the literary world before he joined Uwe Berger's circle.
As early as February 1982, the Main Division XX/7 sent out the
first of a series of letters to the Guards Regiment, enquiring about
the teenager: 'hostile persons' and 'oppositionally suspect writers',
such as the great novelist Stefan Heym, had apparently met Ruika
at readings and literary parties and taken a shine to the talented
youngster. The Stasi's central information service was tasked with
scrutinising his background and connections. The initial verdict
was positive: because of his mother's literary activities, Ruika
was familiar with the Biermann saga and had 'learnt to differ-
entiate'. Uwe Berger's first reports on his poetry had raised some
questions about the purity of his ideological convictions, but by
September 1983, there were signs of improvement. Ruika, Berger
wrote in one dispatch, 'seems to be making good progress': 'He is
prepared to change and gets involved.' Earlier in the year he had
married his girlfriend and become a father for the first time. 'He
seems relaxed,' Berger felt. On 13 September, Ruika was officially
designated a potential future recruit, a 'probationary' unofficial
informant, complete with the provisional cover name 'Grosse'.
Over the coming months, he was invited eight times for meetings
at an apartment in Marzahn, where a man from the Stasi asked

him questions about people he knew and told him to make more enquiries about various people he didn't. The reports on these meetings in his file are vaguely phrased, but suggest that in some cases Ruika complied. In others he didn't. Ruika was 'not an easy character', Berger commented. 'I'm on the right path / and try to be nice / and share all day and night', goes a verse in one of the young Chekist's poems. 'But still / I fight.'

One tactic the Stasi deployed when it couldn't land a catch that was thrashing about wildly under the surface was to stun it with a swift blow. In late summer 1984, Alexander Ruika was ordered to make a delivery from his command post at Erkner to the main compound in Adlershof. His holiday was due to start the day after, and he had again been invited to attend the Poetry Seminar in Schwerin. But after he dropped off the parcel at the post room, the guard at the front gate would not let him leave. After Ruika tried to start a fight, he was thrown in a cell, where he embarked on a hunger strike in protest. Three days in, when hunger and thirst started to bite, his cell door opened and a woman in her forties entered. 'I think there are some problems here we need to talk about,' she said, and Ruika opened up, telling her about his marriage problems, the burden of becoming a father, his conflicts with his parents and his ambivalence about working for the Ministry for State Security. The woman listened patiently, but after an hour her demeanour suddenly changed: she told Ruika that he was a bad person set on boycotting life in the GDR, an enemy of socialism who deserved to be locked up in Bautzen, the notoriously rough political prison in Saxony. When Ruika barked back at her, the woman left. After a few days without further questioning, he received a message that another visitor wanted to see him. In the visitor's room at Adlershof, his father was waiting for him, a large peach resting on the table between the two men. Unless he wanted to end up in prison for the long haul, his father said, he needed to apologise. 'Think about it,' the old colonel said. 'Don't be stupid.'

On 19 July 1984, Alexander Ruika's probationary status was upgraded to that of an IMS, an unofficial informant tasked with infiltrating a specific area of public life. His file states that the informant was available for service around the clock – 'in his free time, during the day, at night' – and that he was sent on a mission to create a 'who is who' profile of aspiring young authors in Berlin and Leipzig, as well as making close observations of public readings by authors suspected of dissident tendencies. Sometimes cadre files will hint that an informant was blackmailed into service – the phrase 'making amends' is a giveaway. Ruika's file at least claims that the young man took on his new task of his own free will, because 'he recognises the necessity of our secret struggle'.

When his military service came to an end in September that year and he left his barracks for the last time, Alexander Ruika was unofficial collaborator 'IM Michael Lindner', his name possibly a fatalistic nod to Michael Lindener, a sixteenth-century author of bawdy broadsides who appointed himself 'poeta laureatus' of Leipzig and was executed for stabbing an innkeeper to death.

I looked back over Ruika's poems. There was one called 'Transformation in Autumn, or The Call-Up', which describes the crossing of a symbolic threshold. 'Close the door / and walk. / Far. How far?' The first time I read this poem I had detected a bitter after-taste, a sarcastic undertone: I imagined Ruika was subverting the language of conscription to describe what was actually his departure from the Guards Regiment, stepping out into the real world. But now I wasn't so sure: maybe the poet was walking in rather than out. 'Step through the gate,' the poem concludes. 'Be weak / and /

become strong.' Another Ruika wrote for the poetry circle was called 'In Anger, or: After a Discussion about Literature'.

> Go ahead!
> You keep on searching for your true selves!
> Dig up your own navel,
> immortalise the sighs of your bedfellows
> Go ahead.
> Meanwhile I go out into the world
> TO THE GIANT OF MUROM
> I want to wake him.

Who was this giant, so awesome he required capitalisation? I emailed a folk-tale specialist I knew, who referred me to a Russian historian, who said he hadn't heard of the Giant of Murom but would put my query to an email group of Slavicists. A Swiss academic pointed me towards a poem by Rainer Maria Rilke, 'The Tsars', that referred to the waking of 'Ilya, the Giant of Murom'. Another email, this time from a scholar in the US: the Giant of Murom was Ilya Muromets, a mythical knight errant of medieval Russian epic poetry, who defended the medieval kingdom of Rus against foreign invaders. She pointed me to a recently published book. Ten years after the fall of the Berlin Wall, in 1999, the Russian Orthodox Church went on to make Ilya Muromets the patron saint of Russian border guards. His most famous epic adventure was the battle with Solovei the Brigand. 'Solovei' is the Russian word for nightingale, the bird that poets through the ages have identified as avian kin to their own profession: 'A Poet is a nightingale, who sits in darkness and sings to cheer its own solitude with sweet sounds,' wrote Shelley. But Solovei the Brigand was not a sweet-sounding bird but a monster, half-human, half-animal, who had a human family and a human face, but could also fly and lived in a tree. His special skill was not a sweet night song but a high-pitched shriek that made flowers lose their petals and devastated entire cities. If someone were really to wake the Giant of Murom, then the old Russian folk tale warned that he would take his revenge on the poets:

> Then the old Cossack Ilya Muromets
> Quickly mounted his good steed,
> He took Nightingale to the open field
> And he cut off his reckless head.

Lesson 9

DISSONANCE

A disruption of harmonic sounds or rhythms;
a harsh collection of sounds.

Inside the impregnable fortress at Adlershof, a vague feeling was growing that something outside its gates wasn't right. Stray signals were finding their way through the Stasi's impenetrable walls and showing up on their radars. Some inside picked up incomprehensible static noise, interspersed with clearly audible messages spelling doom and destruction. Björn Vogel reflected on world affairs in a stream-of-consciousness poem.

His poetic self is disorientated and deprived of sleep: night is day and day is night. An alarm clock wakes him in the dark. He puts on a fresh shirt and reads the news in a trance. All is a blur: news stories, readers' letters and TV listings run into one another. The flavour of imminent apocalypse is discernible: 'Match reports state visits plague of locusts'. A headline catches Vogel's attention, and a chill runs down his spine: a lightning strike has triggered the firing of three American rockets from their missile silos.

A line break indicates a sigh of relief: they are only 'meteorological rockets', not designed to sow death and destruction but to harvest information about wind and the weather.

The Stasi poetry circle no longer produced love poems about Marx, Lenin or their girlfriends. Current affairs had gripped the minds of the Chekist bards. A sergeant-major wrote an ode to Christel Guillaume, the 'weak / strong wife' of the heroic Stasi spy who recently returned to the GDR after spending eleven years in a

West German prison, for the crime of infiltrating the ruling Social Democratic Party. Alexander Ruika wrote a poem in free verse called 'Belafonte 83', about the Jamaican-born crooner who had criticised the US invasion of Grenada at a concert in East Berlin's Palace of the Republic earlier in the year: 'His pain / turned strength / and infected / us all.' The year 1984 would prove pivotal, and not only for Ruika. Gerd Knauer, the young propaganda officer, sensed atmospheric turbulence, a brewing storm: the political weather was changing. 'You can feel it, more and more / history's summer season's at the door', he wrote in 'Summer'.

Apocalypse was not just a vague fear haunting the lyrical outpourings of the Stasi poets but a game being planned by military commanders on either side of the Iron Curtain. Forty years after the Allied liberation of continental Europe from Nazi rule, another full-scale war was looming, and the damage and loss of civilian life would be far greater than the last time around. That much had been clear since NATO forces had acted out a highly realistic war game across Western Europe in November 1983. Involving the deployment of sixteen thousand additional troops to the continent, technicians rolling out realistic-looking dummy warheads, actual ministers communicating via ciphered messages, and even cooperation between state leaders like Margaret Thatcher and Helmut Kohl, the 'Able Archer' exercise had simulated what would happen if a hypothetical opponent, known as 'Orange', employed chemical weapons against NATO member states. According to a debriefing document composed after the exercise was over, two days of 'low spectrum conventional play' would have been followed by three days of 'high spectrum nuclear warfare'.

'Able Archer' had only been a hypothetical drill, but it made the possibility of a nuclear war on European soil seem all too real. In

West Germany, fear of nuclear Armageddon had done nothing less than reset the Federal Republic's political compass. A centre-left West German Chancellor, of all people, had played a part in bringing East–West relations back down to the frosty settings of the 1960s. At a security conference in London in 1977, Social Democrat Helmut Schmidt had drawn attention to two hundred SS-20 missiles positioned on Soviet territory as part of a Russian weapons upgrade programme. Known in the Soviet Union as RSD-10 Pioneer, the SS-20 was a mobile missile with three warheads and a range of more than 2,500 kilometres – making the entire Western half of the continent a potential target. Within two years, Schmidt's warning led to the NATO 'double-track' decision, the first track being an offer of negotiating a ban of middle-range nuclear missiles, and the second track being the threat of matching the build-up in the East with more missiles in West Germany if negotiations failed, which they did. Although the Soviet Union moved quickly to withdraw twenty thousand soldiers and a thousand tanks from East Germany, the missiles remained – US experts speculated there were warheads positioned near East Berlin. By 1982, the political climate in the West German capital, Bonn, had become tense: Helmut Schmidt lost a no-confidence vote and had to watch his own party turn against NATO's double-track decision. In March 1983, the Green Party entered the Bundestag for the first time. That October, some 1.3 million West Germans took to the streets to protest against the nuclear arms race, the biggest demonstration of the post-war era at the time. With negotiations with the Soviet Union still at a standstill in November, the West German Bundestag voted by 286 to 226 to allow the US to station Pershing II and Tomahawk cruise missiles in southern Germany. A day later, Soviet leaders walked out of the talks. In the West German press, there were reports of even more modern nuclear missiles, the SS-22, being moved to East Germany and the Bohemian Forest. All the most dangerous pieces in a giant game of Cold War missile chess were pointing to Berlin in the middle of the board, while America and Russia's kings were safely barricaded in at the top and bottom. West Germany was the obvious target for a pre-emptive nuclear strike by the Soviets, while East Germany was most likely to take the first hit from retaliatory NATO action – and vice versa. If a lightning strike were to trigger a missile launcher, or a passenger plane was to be mistaken for a spy mission, as had happened with the downed Korean Air Lines Flight 007 in September 1983, then it didn't really matter who cast the first stone: burning German cities would have been the end result. 'Instead of creating a more secure situation,' *Spiegel* magazine wrote in February 1984, criticising the Bonn coalition government, 'they have led both German states into a dead end of ever greater danger.'

Were nightmares east of the Iron Curtain plagued by buzzing warheads too? US President Ronald Reagan put that question to the American ambassador to the Soviet Union on 28 March 1984: 'Do you think Soviet leaders really fear us, or is all the huffing and puffing just part of their propaganda?' he asked. The American leader knew that for the last three years the Soviet Union had started to look closely for early indicators of an impending nuclear strike from the West via Operation RYaN, a joint move by the KGB and the military intelligence directorate, GRU, the 'Main Directorate of the General Staff of the Armed Forces of the Russian Federation'. Frantic activity around Western European military bases was causing sweaty palms in the Kremlin, where Brezhnev's death in 1982 had left a power vacuum that neither of his short-term successors, Yuri Andropov and Konstantin Chernenko, had been able to fill. As 'Able Archer' commenced, the Kremlin issued instructions for a dozen aircraft in Eastern Germany and Poland to be fitted with nuclear weapons. Around seventy SS-20 missiles were placed on heightened alert. Soviet nuclear submarines had dived under Arctic ice to avoid detection. One CIA asset on the Eastern side of the Iron Curtain, a Czechoslovakian intelligence officer, tried to impress upon the men around Ronald Reagan that there was genuine fear behind the huffing and puffing in the East. Senior figures in Soviet intelligence, he noted, were 'obsessed' with the historical echoes of 1941, the year Nazi Germany invaded the Soviet Union in a surprise attack that caught Stalin off guard.

But East German leaders were less scared, or at least less willing to admit to their own fears. Markus Wolf, the Stasi's spymaster and son of the GDR diplomat and 'art as weapon' philosopher Friedrich Wolf, noticed the increasingly urgent demand for nuclear-related intelligence from Moscow with concern. East Germany's Soviet partners, Colonel General Wolf worried, had become 'obsessed with the danger of a nuclear missile attack'. Watching the A-bomb play havoc with the political landscape in West Germany had made East German leaders cautious. Because while there were no political opposition parties in the East German parliament, there were stirrings of a home-grown peace movement, largely organised by the Protestant church. A manifesto by the preacher Rainer Eppelmann and the communist Robert Havemann called on the Socialist Unity Party to stop the 'production, sale and import' of arms, replace military service with 'social peace service' for conscientious objectors, and give up its expensive penchant for military parades. The movement even had its own logo and motto, 'Swords to Ploughshares', which managed not only to quote the Bible but also to invert the motto of the Ministry for State Security, the 'shield and sword of the Party'. A delegation of newly elected West German Green Party politicians wore the logo on their shirts as they met with General Secretary Erich Honecker in November 1983.

The Stasi pulled badges with the logo off young people's jackets whenever they could – a pointless measure, because many protesters moved to deliberately cutting round holes into the arms of their jackets to show their allegiance. In its insistence not to show any weakness in the Cold War game of chicken, East Germany was starting to look less agile and even more stubborn than the Soviet Union. Honecker did not want to know about an East German peace movement because the *Little Political Dictionary* had made very clear that the global peace movement was directed against the 'military–industrial complex of the USA and other imperialist states'. To support peace meant to support the Socialist Unity Party. The use of modern weapons of mass destruction, the dictionary had ascertained, was something advocated solely by the Western powers: 'The USSR and all other peace-loving powers are fighting for a ban on the production, dissemination and use of weapons of mass destruction, and their destruction over the course of gradual disarmament.' No footnote to the entry mentioned that the Soviet Union's stockpile of nuclear warheads had been outgrowing that of the US since 1978.

In the Stasi, fear of nuclear war accentuated a generational divide. The NATO two-track decision, the SS-20s and the new Pershings on the other side of the Wall had been debated among officers at the biannual skill enhancement camp in the spring. As at every camp, there had been rifle drills and target practice, and in the evening junior and senior Stasi officers sat by the campfire and shot the breeze. An older officer in his mid-sixties spoke up and told the younger cadres not to wet their pants. The war might blow everything to smithereens, he said, but in the end there were always a couple of people who managed to crawl out of their holes afterwards and build up a new world from scratch. Knauer, the young propaganda officer, was quietly seething with rage: East Germany was a touch of a button away from all-out nuclear war, and his colleagues thought they could just 'crawl out of their holes' afterwards. He wanted to tell the older officer to his face what consequences a nuclear war on German soil would have, but when surrounded by Stasi officers you had to be careful what you said. In the coming weeks, Knauer channelled his anger and frustration into his typewriter.

At first, the thirty-one-year-old embarked on a draft of a science fiction manuscript about two warring planets in the same solar system who both develop a super-weapon. But the novel ended up in the bin. Instead, Knauer started a poem with the title 'The Bang': poetry allowed you to say more by saying less. Page one starts with an idyllic scene, like in one of Brecht's love poems. The narrator is basking in the sunshine on a meadow full of daisies, dreaming of 'a pair of women's breasts': 'Summer is a giant / I am a dwarf / snugly shielded in its palm'. At the top of page three, there's suddenly a noise as loud 'as a thunderclap', followed by a blinding white light, 'daggers stabbing into your pupils'. Something is wrong, the narrator realises: the world is 'hovering / on a precipice'. Doomsday is coming. Knauer poured forth feelings he wasn't usually allowed to express to his comrades. Across two full pages, he described 'the fear / that everything might end', 'fear / of the explosions', 'fear of those / that think themselves god's warriors', 'fear of those that stand to profit / from this madness in our world', 'fear that something – by mistake – / will not go to plan', 'fear that more people will burn / than have ever burned before'. The young poet wrote himself into a rage. Locked into an ABAB rhyme scheme, the poem picks up pace, jumping from the personal to the political, tumbling from the political to the biblical, falling from the biblical to the mythical. By page ten, the poem is narrated by Odysseus, running in terror through 'the fog of history'. Odysseus meets Prometheus, who bursts into tears in the face of the nuclear apocalypse, and cries: 'That's not what I wanted / The fire was meant to save you.' Hounded by rolling thunder, Odysseus flees further, into the ivory tower where the philosophers live, seeking spiritual guidance in this hour of need. But Plato, Hegel and Kant all remain silent. Only a man with a bushy beard rises from his seat with an apologetic look on his face:

Karl Marx tries to make a plea
Looks Odysseus in the face
Says gravely:
They're doing it because of me
But they put their faith in the wrong place.

By page thirteen, the narrator, who at this stage may or may not be Odysseus, is stumbling across a hellscape strewn with dead bodies:

Some naked others wearing clothes,
Some sliced right open from head to toes,
Others without a blemish on their skin
Grabbed by the reaper in a flash,
Some with a horribly distorted grin
Some burnt to charcoal
Others one big bleeding gash.

He sees dead men, women and children, and is harassed by hungry rats.

> I drag myself
> for weeks on end
> and stumble all alone
> no longer through hills of rotting flesh
> but mountains made of bone.

On page sixteen, he meets a group of anti-communist cannibals, who chant 'We've rid the entire periphery / of crimson-red barbarity' before raping women and then dismembering them limb by limb: 'Serve up an arm, a leg, a foot, a toe, / Then smash the head in with one blow.' On page twenty-one, the narrator meets a group of deformed men and women who live off stews made of bugs and flies. A woman with two heads ponders how the green planet she once knew came to be so devastated:

> Who took a stand
> against this ghastly fate?
> Was there too little fear at hand?
> Did fear show up too late?

In June 1984, Gerd Knauer read the entire poem to the poetry circle. When he finished reading, there was a moment of silence. An ashen-faced kitchen worker, who had joined the group for the first time that day, rushed to the toilet. All the remaining eyes in the room were on the circle's artistic leader. Uwe Berger said the poem was very technically advanced, and he was impressed with the skills the Chekists had acquired. The report he filed to his handler on 14 June 1984 was less restrained. 'Gerd Knauer delivers a fifty-two-page poem on the nuclear destruction of mankind. Spreading fear is the main aim, vividly conveyed through the poem's formal smoothness.' The stanza about Prometheus and Karl Marx in particular troubled him. The syntax was ambiguous: when Marx said 'they are doing it because of me', was the 'it' referring to the other philosophers' silence, or to nuclear war? And if the latter, were 'they' Marx's followers or his enemies? 'The question of guilt is not answered unambiguously,' Berger noted in his report. Knauer implied that 'Marx has invented social revolution and is therefore to blame for the imminent annihilation of mankind,' a thesis that amounted to nothing but 'idealism and acceptance of surrender'. At the end of the circle's meeting, Berger had a word with the young propaganda officer. Did Knauer realise that this 'fear poem' was at odds with his ideological mission in the Ministry for State Security? The younger man told him about the encounter with the old officer at the training camp. Berger tried to remind him of the Socialist Unity Party's 'peace strategy', which was to 'establish peace before war is started and before the imperialist system that causes it has been abolished'. But Berger wasn't entirely convinced that the young man was listening: 'Comrade Knauer and his uptight, pig-headed personality,' he signs off his dispatch.

Around the time Alexander Ruika was signed up as an informant on a special mission, Berger's reports began increasingly to focus on Gerd Knauer. On 6 September 1984, he reported that Knauer had told the circle that 'he is not a worker and won't write a poem about being a worker or about workers being in charge', even if that meant 'the workers will chuck him out'. On 25 October, Berger wrote that Knauer had read out a poem about a dream in which he flew a kite that 'escapes from narrow confinement and sails into freedom'. Berger explained that the kite was what poets called a metaphor, and that the poem was a covert call for East German army personnel to cross over to the West. The young propaganda officer was producing new poems at a prodigious rate, and Berger struggled to keep up. On 13 December, Berger wrote to inform his handler of a poem called 'The Yes Sayers', in which Knauer railed against those who were 'never in doubt about their doubts'. Such people made the young poet want to 'throw up'. Knauer interspersed these depth charges in verse form with partisan poetry: his epic, 'The Bang', had ended on the narrator waking from his nightmare on the realisation that 'the fight for peace in our world / needs me / like I need peace.' But Berger was convinced these were diversion tactics, 'an alibi'. He was dealing with a professional sabotage attempt. Knauer, he concluded, was 'systematically obstructing the Circle of Writing Chekists.'

Gerd Knauer agreed to meet me in Marzahn, a district around ten kilometres from the Brandenburg Gate. For Berliners who live in central districts like Mitte, Kreuzberg or Prenzlauer Berg, Marzahn is a cliché, a part of the city full of *Ossis* on low incomes who never wanted or accepted the fall of the Wall. Home to what was once Europe's largest high-rise estate, where 103,000 model apartments were built in the 1970s, many of its streets are ravines flanked by crags of prefab concrete. The Wall, which has vanished from the city as a whole, is literally still at home here, stored by the city senate in neat rows in a backyard of the local botanical gardens, which occasionally hands over segments as gifts on grand state visits. On the way to my meeting, I passed artist Walter

Womacka's recently restored socialist realist 'Peace' mural, and the voices of a choir singing Russian folk songs floated in and out of earshot. But to picture this corner of Berlin as a 'Goodbye Lenin' style bubble in which the sun has never set on the Soviet Union would be misleading. As in many parts of Germany that used to lie east of the Wall, the weeds of late capitalism have sprouted more aggressively in Marzahn than in the protected biotopes of West Berlin. Gerd Knauer had proposed we meet in front of Eastgate, a US-style shopping mall seemingly modelled on a tape dispenser, more vulgar and egregious than anything you would find in genteel Schöneberg or Friedenau.

The propaganda officer's cadre file had painted a picture of a man with an ability to breeze through situations in which his senior comrades were weighed down by dogma. Born 2 August 1952 in Chemnitz, Knauer was a stand-out student at school, quick on the uptake and gifted with broad general knowledge. His only flaw, teachers bemoaned, was that he struggled to hide his boredom when he had to wait for fellow pupils to catch up. The file noted that he did not 'cultivate contact with adolescents who embody Western decadence', though there were glimpses of a kind of home-grown exuberance that didn't sound too dissimilar.

After joining the Guards Regiment at nineteen, Knauer was repeatedly ticked off for little incidents that hinted at a lax attitude: he dropped an important key to a safe in the woods before going for a spontaneous dip in a lake, and he accidentally left behind a service card revealing his membership of the secret police in a hotel room. Less mentally agile members of the Stasi would have lost their jobs over such infractions, but Knauer seemed to have floated on. First from the Guards Regiment to a university course in journalism, where he was reprimanded for skipping lessons but

nonetheless passed the final exam with flying colours, and then
back to the Stasi, into the propaganda unit.

The passport photo in Gerd Knauer's cadre file had led me
to expect a person as buttoned-up and tight-lipped as some of
his former circle colleagues. But the trainer-wearing, bestub-
bled man I met outside the Eastgate shopping mall was different:
relaxed, friendly and open to telling stories from his past. Over
a Vietnamese duck curry, Knauer told me how much he had
enjoyed the aftermath of the GDR's collapse, how he had spent
years on the dole writing crime novels, before coming across a
job ad for an agency that helped East Germans file tax returns.
Working in the Stasi meant he had more experience with bureaucracy than ordinary citizens of a state that filled its coffers directly
from nationalised industry rather than taxing personal income.
Many ordinary East Germans had fallen into a deep hole as the
world around them was transformed, unable to cope with the
daily demands of the market economy, terrified of ending up on
the streets. Some senior officers at the Stasi's propaganda unit
had wound up selling newspapers on street corners, others were
unemployed. A former speech-writer of the Stasi chief, Mielke,
was working in a warehouse. Yet Knauer had simply cruised from
the old ideological system into the new. Working at the agitation and propaganda unit had cushioned the culture shock, he
explained. The department's archives in Johannisthal held not
only Western spy thrillers, but also action movies and porn films.
Writers and artists dropped by regularly, and employees thought
of themselves as bohemians rather than bureaucrats. Compared
to the radio station where Knauer had done an internship after
his university course, working for the Stasi was a boon for his
work-life balance, with few urgent deadlines and casual working

hours. Business trips were quickly approved and rarely checked. He was able to acquire and find time to read books that weren't available in bookshops, and developed a growing admiration for the poetry of Wolf Biermann, the singer-songwriter whom his employer had worked so hard to hound out of the country. Biermann, he said, was a master of his craft. Of course he didn't completely approve of his politics at the time, but there was much to be admired in his poetry: subtle humour, the ability to criticise things that deserved criticising in a way that was as intelligent as it was insidious. What did he think of the poems of Uwe Berger, the poetry circle leader, I asked. Knauer ordered a second beer. Hard to digest, he said. Almost illegible. Too much content, too little poetry. Poetry, said Knauer, was the sound of a little bird, singing. But Berger didn't want to hear birdsong, he wanted every poem to sound like the Internationale.

The good poem as a miniature model for the good society: at the outset of the Stasi poetry circle, that had once been the idealistic vision. A state with steady feet and a perfectly calibrated rhyme structure would learn to wind its way through the corridor of history to the steady beat of thesis, antithesis and synthesis, just as the sonnet unfurls down the page. But by 1984 it wasn't just thanks to the dissonant chords struck by Gerd Knauer's poems that the state was starting to lose its rhythm. As the atom bomb grew larger in the minds of ordinary East Germans, cracks also started to show in the Adlershof compound. An internal report, published in March 1984, tried to get to the bottom of a noticeable decline in morale inside the *Wachregiment*. In the preceding twelve months, there had been a disconcerting rise in disciplinary measures against Feliks Dzerzhinsky guards, in response to fights between personnel inside barracks or members of the regiment getting drunk and lashing out at civilians. An increasing number of new recruits were expressing their displeasure at the number of hours they were required to train and the hardship involved. One likely factor behind this shift in attitude, the report concluded, was the rising consumption of Western means of mass communication. Many East German officers openly admitted to watching West German TV, 'because the television of the GDR only provides youth-appropriate entertainment shows of insufficient quality and quantity'. 'Watching films and sport shows is now commonplace,' the report concluded resignedly. The lack of information about political events was frequently cited as a reason for switching off East Germany's state broadcasters.

In keeping with the Bitterfeld ethos of opening up literature to the masses, the barracks had its own library for soldiers of all ranks, and in this library there was also a shelf full of vinyl records that was sporadically updated with new releases. New additions to the Feliks Dzerzhinsky record collection in September 1985 included an album by East Berlin band Karat, an anthology of marching songs called 'The Boys from Moscow and Berlin', as well as a compilation of 'Red Songs' that contained an updated version of Ernst Busch's popular anti-American ditty 'Ami Go Home', sung to the tune of 'Tramp! Tramp! Tramp!': 'Ami collect your Pershings in a haste / Pershings are a bloody waste,' the lyrics went, 'Go home, Ami! Ami go home / split your atoms for peace instead.' Yet whoever had been in charge of ordering new stock that month hadn't exactly taken the spirit of the song to heart. Apart from albums by Eric Clapton, Joe Cocker and Roxy Music, acquisitions in September also included a Foreigner 'Best Of' and Michael Jackson's *Thriller*. Twenty years earlier, the then president of the Socialist Unity Party, Walter Ulbricht, had insisted that East

Germany should not 'copy every piece of dirt that comes from the West' and should take a stand against the 'monotony of the Yeah Yeah Yeah' of the Beatles. Now, behind the fortified walls at Adlershof, soldiers were suddenly staring into the distance while listening to 'I Want to Know What Love Is' and clicking their fingers in time to 'Billy Jean'.

Something similar was happening at the cinema where East Germany's elite military force was allowed to unwind in front of the big screen. Since 1981, senior officials had allowed the projectionists to show not just agitprop classics from Russia, Romania and Cuba, but also the odd movie from a capitalist country. The only proviso: someone needed to keep attendance records and monitor audience numbers for the two ideological categories. The results were worrying indeed: even though almost twice as many soldiers and spies flooded into the auditorium for capitalist films as early as 1981, the numbers began to grow out of all proportion. In the year 1984–85, there were on average 623 viewers for each capitalist production compared to 211 for each film from socialist brother states, even though capitalist movies only made up about a tenth of the programme. The popularity of some of these films wasn't surprising: the animated feature film *The Twelve Tasks of Asterix*, for example, told the story of a little town surrounded by outposts of an evil Roman empire, striking a chord with the military personnel, even if it premiered in Adlershof almost ten years after its release in the West. In René Goscinny and Albert Uderzo's film, Caesar challenges Asterix and Obelix to a series of Herculean tasks in order to disprove rumours of their godlike powers – only to watch the two Gauls repeatedly beat the odds and come up trumps. To East Germans, whose Olympic team had finished in the top three of the medal table in every summer Olympics it had participated in, even beating the mighty United States to second place in Montreal 1976, watching this light-hearted adventure story triggered a warm glow of recognition. Senior officials in the Ministry for State Security might have also appreciated how non-judgementally this French box-office hit depicted the use of performance-enhancing magic potions: in 1974, the Ministry had overseen a large state-sponsored doping programme, 'State Plan Theme 14–25', which involved around twelve thousand athletes being treated with untested steroids or male hormones, some of them without their knowledge and most of them unaware of the physical and psychological consequences. Those placed lower down the chain of command could find solace in Asterix and Obelix's eighth task, where the two Gauls have to enter a multi-storey government building, The House that Sends You Mad, to obtain a permit. Driven to the edge of insanity by an illogical and inhumane bureaucratic apparatus, the heroes managed to complete their challenge only after they beat their opponents with their own weapons, inventing a fictional 'Permit Number A39, stipulated in Circular B65' that sets the officials off on a wild goose chase culminating in collective madness among the bureaucrats and the handing out of the desired permit.

If the Asterix movie could still be explained away as a glorified depiction of how socialism in one village can go on to beat the world, the inclusion of a genuine Hollywood blockbuster on the programme of the Adlershof regiment's on-site cinema in February 1985 comes as more of a shock. Steven Spielberg's *Close Encounters of the Third Kind* had originally been released in the West eight years before, but its message had gained a new urgency after Reagan declared the USSR the 'evil empire' and announced a new missile defence system that was soon known as 'Star Wars'. In the movie, Richard Dreyfus plays Roy Neary, a blue-collar electrician who is haunted by visions and daydreams after a close encounter with a UFO; a five-tone leitmotif, written by *Jaws* composer John Williams, plays in the heads of anyone who has had a glimpse of extraterrestrial life. But if science fiction films before and after portrayed alien life-forms from the other side as many-tentacled, blood-sucking invaders, Spielberg's 1977 film shows them to be kind-hearted creatures with angelic voices. The film's narrative runs on the conventional Hollywood fuel of rugged individualism: its dominant conflict is not between ordinary humans and alien visitors, but between human individuals and the officials who try to contain them, such as employers, politicians and military authorities. Its central question, however, implies a strongly pacifist viewpoint: what if, the film asked, the gigantic strange object falling from the sky was not an ending to be feared, but the beginning of something? 'Stop and be friendly,' says a sign that one UFO truther holds up when he sees lights descending from the night sky: a thoroughly counter-intuitive message to beam into the heads of military personnel on the borderline of a brewing nuclear conflict in the middle of the new Cold War.

Close Encounters of the Third Kind was an odd film to screen inside Adlershof in 1985. Not just because of its laissez-faire attitude to the enemy from the other side, or because it would once have been considered a weapon in the culture war, but also because it already predicted how that culture war would eventually be won: not with nuclear weapons, but by sending pop-song melodies, lines of poetry and film scenes across the Iron Curtain, which would embed themselves in minds as if by telekinesis. In February 1985, the Stasi agents inside the Adlershof cinema were not just watching Roy Neary's quest to reach out to another world, they were also becoming little GDR Roys, already transfixed by music from the other side. As US and Soviet leaders ratcheted up their rhetoric and Europe cowered in fear of the big bang, there was a new spirit of détente inside the very place where Feliks Dzerzhinsky's cool head, hot heart and clean hands were meant to rule supreme.

Lesson 10

PALINODE

An ode or song that retracts or recants what the poet wrote in a previous poem.

The black Volga was waiting under the street lamp in silence, as if its wheels had never moved an inch. Only the pulse of the yellow taxi sign on its roof throbbed through the December smog. Gert Neumann stumbled the few steps across the icy pavement. The chrome handle was cold to the touch, even through woolly gloves. Neumann pulled the back door shut and sank deep into the synthetic leather. Where was he off to, the driver asked from the front seat. Neumann hesitated for a minute. He hadn't really thought about that until now. Then he made up his mind. Let's go all the way to Leipzig. From East Berlin to Leipzig, East Germany's second-largest city, it was easily a three-hour drive. Neumann had never taken a taxi all the way before, but tonight he was too exhausted for the train. Was 100 Deutsche Mark enough, he asked. Earlier in 1987, East Germany's central bank had printed so much money that the exchange rate had briefly gone through the roof: for the first time ever, one Deutsche Mark got you ten of its GDR equivalents. But there was no need for Neumann to spell out the conversion rate. The taxi was already moving.

Of all the enemies the Stasi had racked up among East Germany's literary scene, Gert Neumann was the most confusing. Forty-five years old but looking fifty-plus, he had first got into trouble with the state in 1968, with a poetry reading on a boat on Leipzig's Elsterstausee lake that had included citations from Alexander Dubček's 'Action Programme', the Czechoslovak communist politician's plan for an independent path to socialism. After being chucked out of university, Neumann and his wife, the poet Heidemarie Härtl, had developed a manifesto for a new type of literature. At the core of their vision was the belief that the Socialist Unity Party had, through monotonous decrees, jargon engineered at Party conferences and lies printed in state-sponsored newspapers, so thoroughly corrupted the common language of the people of East Germany as to render it useless. 'The dictatorship of black words', Neumann wrote, had 'murdered' poetry. To describe the world truthfully again, poets needed to first go into hiding. Neumann did not take an overtly political stance in his writing, nor did he try to emulate Western literary idols. What made his work provocative to the East German state was that it was so cryptic that even the three literary critics the Culture Ministry hired to analyse his texts couldn't work out exactly what he was trying to say. Neumann was a locksmith by trade, and he wrote like one. His first two novels, *Guilty Words* and *Eleven O'Clock*, were like locked rooms with keys gone missing: little plot, little direct speech, few individuated characters, long labyrinthine sentences, a dense thicket of literary quotations and references. 'The collective of individualities has a silent interest in dissolving potential intelligence into a dumb and blind form of observation,' he wrote in *Eleven O'Clock*. Sentences like these were so elusive, so hard to pin down, that they drove some of his silent observers into a fury. Uwe Berger, the Stasi poetry circle's poet-spy-in-chief, described Gert Neumann in one of his reports as 'a semi-educated psychopath', whose 'confused thoughts' and 'highfalutin gibberish' rejected life in the socialist republic and 'propagated a religious irrationalism'.

Neumann's books weren't published in East Germany, but they weren't officially censored either: his manuscripts simply got stuck in the state censor's office because even the Culture Ministry's smartest minds couldn't figure out what they actually said. Eventually, he lost patience and posted the manuscripts of his first two books across the border in chunks, where the two books were picked up by Fischer, the biggest literary publishing house in West Germany. As a result, no one in the East could read Gert Neumann, but West German writers and critics adored him. The influential West German novelist Martin Walser, one of his biggest champions, bumped into the East German Culture Minister at a hotel in Leipzig and told him that Neumann had such force that he would defeat them all: 'If you are against this human being,' Walser said, 'then you've already lost!'

To confuse the Stasi even further, Neumann showed no apparent interest in acting like the enemy of state they made him out to be. He had personally considered Walser's intervention highly unhelpful, because the last thing he wanted was to jump ship to the capitalist West. He believed in solidarity, and William Blake's dictum that opposition is true friendship. Living in a socialist state had taught him things about humanity he didn't think he could experience as a refugee to the West. Neumann wrote *Eleven O'Clock* while working full-time as a locksmith at a large department store in Leipzig. Every day at 11 a.m., Neumann had put down his spanner and picked up his pen to describe short episodes from his working life and muse about poetry. The book would later be regarded by West German critics as a defining work of dissident literature, but in many ways it was literature as the founding fathers of the socialist GDR had envisioned it: art made by working people, for working people, among working people.

'Pick up the quill, comrade,' as Walter Ulbricht had once put it. The 'separation between art and life', the 'alienation between artists and the people' that the Socialist Unity Party had spent the last forty years worrying about – Neumann had found his own strategy to overcome it long ago. He had created a social reality, much more social and a hundred times more real than the socialist realism decreed by the state.

At Mühlenbeck, to the north of the city, the taxi joined the ring road to orbit West Berlin counterclockwise. The car stereo was playing jazz, but the road was thumping its own rhythm over the blue notes. Da-dong. Da-dong. Da-dong. The Volga was usually a smooth ride: a heavy barge of a car with a three-speed gearbox and an outline that mimicked that of a classic American cruiser. East Germans nicknamed the car *Bonzenschaukel* or 'fat cats' swing'. But the Berlin ring road was bumpy, still made up of the same concrete plates the Nazis had laid down during the Third Reich five decades ago. Over the years, the weight of traffic had gradually pushed the segments apart and you could feel each gap through the Volga's suspension. Da-dong. The even stretch between each bump was just about long enough for the car to start swaying. Da-dong. Neumann's back was killing him. At work, they called him 'the hunchback of Notre-Dame' because his posture was so bad. The doctors said it was a mystery illness: tension in the back and neck, triggered by mental stress. If only the bloody springs in this back seat weren't so worn through. He squinted to make out the features of the man in the seat in front of him, but the glow of the street lamps was too weak. Da-dong. Perhaps once they made it past Potsdam he would get a few sweet minutes' shut-eye.

In 1987, more than three thousand people successfully plotted their escape across the border into West Germany. Thousands more dreamt up plans that were dashed by bad timing, the watchful eyes of a border guard or simply their own lack of courage. Neumann, however, had just spent the last six months agonising over whether he would be able to cross the border in the other direction. In June he had accepted a string of invitations in Western Europe: one engagement in Amsterdam, another in Rolandseck, near Bonn. But in the West every interview, every dinner party, every reading had seemed like a trap. There was the room in Laren outside Amsterdam he was accused of having wrecked after staying there for a few nights, the provocative questions from the audience at a reading inside the disused train station, dotted with the jargon of the Stasi cadres: all these incidents, he was convinced, had been engineered to trigger a scandal the Party could use as grounds to refuse him re-entry into the East. Yet he had dodged them all, and made it back across the border. And now he was as tired as a dog.

There was only one more thing he still needed to sort out, and he had to make his way to Leipzig to do so. His wife Heidemarie had travelled back with him across the border, but then suddenly disappeared for a week. When she returned, she couldn't really explain where she had been. Friends of Neumann's had implied that there was something suspicious about his wife's behaviour. Her father was an army major, after all. So after a few weeks Neumann had told her to leave. You are a nuisance to me, please go back, he had said. She said something in response, but he hadn't understood what she meant. Upon his return to East Berlin, Neumann had stayed for a few days at his son's flat on Linienstrasse. It was here that he came to the conclusion that he needed to travel to Leipzig to meet his wife and break up with her.

He put his sleepy hot head against the cold window. You're in luck, said the driver. I know this journey like the back of my hand.

I used to drive between Berlin and Leipzig all the time when I was studying literature there.

Suddenly, Neumann was wide awake.

———

I had come across Gert Neumann's name in the Stasi archive early on in my research: according to files I had seen, he was one of a handful of writers on whom Alexander Ruika was tasked to gather intelligence after his recruitment as an unofficial informant. A report dated 17 December 1987 mentions an encounter between Neumann and 'Michael Lindner', in which the informant managed to ascertain that the novelist had fallen out with his wife after hearing that she might have spied on him for the Stasi. Citing Ruika as a source, the report claims that Neumann intended to leave the GDR but wanted to make financial preparations first. 'When he leaves, he won't be going quietly,' the report claims. But when I called Gert Neumann in the summer of 2016 to find out if he remembered the encounter with his spy, he shrugged me off: there must be a misunderstanding, Neumann mumbled, and at any rate he wasn't feeling well at the moment. The line went dead.

Neumann's instinctive distrust was understandable. The disciplinary procedure following the nautical poetry reading on Elsterstausee had resulted in a full-scale surveillance operation involving at least seven informants dedicated to tracking his movements. In 1975, the Stasi had broken into Neumann's apartment when he was out, installed bugging devices, photographed every inch and photocopied every piece of paper it could get its hands on. Postal deliveries were intercepted. The Stasi sat in on every train journey, every reading he gave in friends' living rooms.

It tracked every movement of Neumann's curtains and counted every beer he drank in the bar around the corner. A friend of the family was signed up to spy on the novelist and his wife on their holidays. Then, when the Stasi felt it still wasn't watching Neumann closely enough, it simply recruited his own mother to spy on him.

The psychological toll of these surveillance measures was not an accidental side effect. In the early years of the GDR, political dissidents were suppressed mainly via official, legal channels. After the building of the Wall, however, the state tried to clean up its image, declaring its commitment to human rights by signing the 1972 Basic Treaty and the 1975 Helsinki Accords. From then on, any moves against real or imagined enemies of the socialist state needed to take place 'silently'. A 1976 directive by the Stasi head, Erich Mielke, proposed a catalogue of methods of psychological warfare called *Zersetzung* – a scientific term that literally refers to the chemical process of corrosion, but which would nowadays be best translated as gaslighting. Enemies of the state, Mielke instructed, should have their reputation 'systematically discredited' by spreading 'untrue' but 'credible, non-refutable' rumours. To destroy their enemies' confidence, the Stasi would 'systematically organise professional and social disappointments'. In the case of Gert Neumann this meant regular public harassment in the streets, including spot-searches by police and violent assaults. It meant the unexplained arrest of his teenage son and two of his close friends. And it meant the Stasi deliberately tried to sow seeds of doubt in Neumann's mind about his wife's loyalty: one directive advises operatives to 'use existing differences between the married couple' to further 'unsettle' the novelist.

A year after my first phone call I came up with another route to shed light on the encounter between Gert Neumann and Alexander Ruika: perhaps, I thought, there were duplicates of reports missing from the file of the spy that had ended up in the file of the spied upon. The archivist at the Stasi archive said she would need to contact the novelist first to obtain his permission. A week later, she called back: Neumann wanted to talk to me. He had remembered something. We met at Neumann's ground-floor flat in Gesundbrunnen on a sweltering August afternoon. I drank fizzy water, Neumann poured himself a cup of tea with a slice of lemon. His voice was soft, occasionally trailing off into a mumble as he told me about his writing, his family history, the fraught trip to West Germany in 1987, and the taxi journey to Leipzig. It took him about an hour to get to the point: the taxi driver, he was certain, was the Alexander Ruika I was looking for.

His thoughts had started to race as soon as the driver told him that they had grown up in the same Berlin suburb, Hohen-Neuendorf, and that they had studied literature at the same university. To Neumann, this was too much of a coincidence: it had to be a cover, a made-up story designed to get him to feel at ease and talk confidentially. In fact, it did the opposite. Neumann tried to work out how he had ended up in Ruika's car. He had asked his son to call a taxi while he was having a bath – had the phone been bugged? Or did the Stasi have people sitting around in call centres, waiting for a call from the right number? After his son was arrested aged sixteen – officially because of a scuffle outside a youth club – the Stasi had tried to sign him up to spy on his father. He had refused. Or had he? First his mother, then his wife, so why not his son too? But maybe the explanation was much simpler. Maybe this guy in the taxi had just been waiting outside the apartment on spec, and Neumann had unwittingly walked into the lion's den. Earlier in the year, the East German government had legalised the black market in taxis: if you had a car with four doors and a few spare hours after work, you could put a taxi sign on your roof, switch on the state-regulated meter and pick up a couple of passengers. Until then, taxi drivers in East Germany had enjoyed a privileged status thanks to chronic shortages: taxis didn't wait for you, but were waited upon. At Friedrichstrasse station people were used to queueing for several hours. And because the taxi market was as planned as every other part of the economy, drivers had to meet daily quotas and were only allowed to drive ten kilometres between journeys in East Berlin, meaning few drivers wanted to journey too far from the city centre. Now that 'black taxis' were legal, it was easier to book a long-distance trip, but it also meant anyone could be a taxi driver. Sitting behind Ruika, Neumann wished he had looked at the number plate. He knew exactly how to spot a Stasi car. There was a system; you just needed to crack the code. Outside the Leipzig Book Fair there were always Volvos with the numbers three to four. The lower ranks had number plates that always added up to ten. Four fours and it was a Stasi officer. He was sure of it, he told me.

The taxi journey to Leipzig was not the first time Gert Neumann had found himself in a confined space with someone trying to squeeze him for information, and he had a tried-and-tested strategy for moments like these: spamming the system. The aim was to overload his interviewers with information, to give them too much detail to fit into a single report. So Neumann played along with Ruika's questions, railing against the state, talking about the political change that was in the air, openly pondering whether the GDR was heading for inevitable collapse. He used the informal *du*, which he normally hated. Then he tried to turn the tables: so you are a writer too, he asked. He told Ruika he was involved with two literary magazines in Leipzig that always needed fresh blood. How about he submitted a couple of the driver's poems? When they arrived in Leipzig, on Georg-Schwarz-Strasse 118, Neumann handed his driver a copy of his novel *Eleven O'Clock* and a 100 Deutsche Mark note, and told him to keep the change. Before he slammed the car door shut, he said he would be back in Berlin next month to do a reading, at the church on Zionskirchplatz. Why didn't Ruika come along and bring some of his own poems?

To the Stasi, Gert Neumann's philosophical world-view may have been a room behind double-locked doors, but there was also an escape route, a window that let in fresh air. He explained this to me as he poured himself another cup of tea. The East German regime had poisoned the German language to the extent that it was useless to describe the reality of life in the socialist state. But there was something beyond reality: *Wirklichkeit*, or 'realness'. Realness wasn't found in writing but in encounters, in conversations. A conversation was a process that broke down prejudices. After reunification, Neumann had tried to set up a programme that enabled conversations between the oppressors and the victims of the old system, called the 'Workshop for Metals, Texts and Situations', in which people would be encouraged to talk to each other while working together. He'd even received funding from the Saxony Culture Ministry, but the project had fallen at the last hurdle. A conversation is what he had tried to strike up with his spying taxi driver, Alexander Ruika. He thought that may have succeeded. The funny thing, Neumann said as he looked over the photocopies I had made at the Stasi archive, was that Ruika's reports on their taxi journey gave away very little of what was actually said.

It was getting dark. I thanked Neumann for his time and got up to leave. Halfway through the door, I had a thought: how would he feel about meeting up with his spy to continue their conversation? If the proposal came from him rather than me, perhaps Ruika would finally respond? Neumann said he would think about it. A month later I received a letter from Neumann, which he asked me to forward to Ruika: he wanted to invite him to a meeting in Hohen-Neuendorf, the suburb where they had both grown up. The letter was six pages long and included a story about a poisoned orange. Weeks passed, then months. On 12 June 2019, at five minutes to six, just as a thunderstorm was about to break over Berlin, my mobile rang. 'I received a letter from you about a meeting.' It was Ruika.

Driving always came naturally to the young man who had spent his early years teetering between wanting to become a writer or a fighter. Self-doubt evaporated when he sat behind the wheel. Alexander Os Ruika was only fourteen years old when, while his parents were out at work, he took his father's moped for a spin, and he had never looked back. His first car wasn't a bog-standard Trabant or a Wartburg, but an elegant classic DKW Union, built in 1935, which he bought as a wreck for 2,500 Ostmark and nurtured back to life. Some people hire a big band on their wedding day, or splash out on an extravagant meal – when Ruika married in 1983, he borrowed his friend's Volkswagen Mk 1 Golf for the day and sped down Unter den Linden with his bride, Phil Collins blaring out of the car stereo. After his military service in the Guards Regiment had come to an end in 1984, he spent a year jobbing as a driver for the Free German Trade Union Federation, East Germany's sole trade union, where his talent behind the wheel didn't go unnoticed. Sometimes he heard foreign visitors sing his praises in Russian or English from the back seats: what kind of driver this is, they said, so smooth! He had a knack for sensing how far you could push a car before it started to groan, how to take a corner at speed without losing your grip on the road.

Out of the driving seat, uncertainty set in. In 1985, Ruika took up one of the few and sought-after places at Leipzig's prestigious Institute for Literature, where the Stasi wanted to use him to keep tabs on the next generation of literary troublemakers. But he soon got bored sitting in university halls listening to lectures on aesthetics and stopped turning up to classes. In his work as an informant, too, he was soon proving himself to be an unreliable asset, skipping meetings until the Stasi withdrew its protecting hand and Alexander Ruika was thrown off his university course. Naturally, he started driving again, this time for the taxi office in Weissensee, and when he zig-zagged through Berlin at night, he was at ease again. On a good week, the pay was decent: for long-distance trips customers paid for the outbound and the inbound journey, so he could earn 300 Ostmark for three hundred kilometres. And if you were really lucky, you ended up with someone like Gert Neumann on the back seat, who was happy to pay you a bit extra, just because he could.

Ruika had agreed to meet at a Greek restaurant with an outdoor terrace, and the grey-haired man in his late fifties was already at his table by the time we arrived, suspiciously eyeing us from behind a pack of blue Gauloises and a steaming cup of green tea. It was a warm summer evening and the restaurant was busy. Our table was within earshot of the neighbouring guests, but a large family reunion was drawing most of the attention. There was some awkwardness after we had shaken hands and sat down: Neumann began by telling us a confusing anecdote that stumbled from the Brothers Grimm to an encounter with an owl in a country house in France, and from the ancient Romans' belief in domestic deities to the French word for a spy, *mouchard*. Neumann was spamming the system. His story lasted around half an hour, during which I watched Ruika's eyes grow wide with something akin to either bewilderment or panic. We ordered some food, and the atmosphere around the table became more relaxed as Ruika explained how he had ended up as a taxi driver after Adlershof. But then Neumann looked up from his grilled goat's cheese to look Ruika in the eye: I believe the secret police wanted to know what state I was in, and you were meant to find out on that taxi journey, he said. Neumann was a good interviewer.

Ruika said he was struggling to remember every detail of their journey. He paused, and lit another cigarette. One of the best-paid gigs for taxi drivers in East Berlin was the pick-up at Hotel Metropol just by Friedrichstrasse station, a five-star lodging which drew visitors from around the world and was rumoured to have the best prostitutes in town. But competition for the gig was stiff, and every time there was a call-out for drivers near Friedrichstrasse from the head office at Weissensee, someone else seemed to get the job. One day a friend had tipped him off about a mechanic who could boost the signal on his radio for a bung, and the next time Ruika responded to a Friedrichstrasse call-out, his call-back jumped other drivers and got him the job. But in hindsight he wondered whether maybe the stronger signal also made it easier for HQ to listen in on what was going on inside his taxi: was he driving a bugging device on four wheels? There was a microphone next to the speaker on his dashboard: what if the mechanic had made sure it was on the whole time? And what if the Stasi simply put one of their men into the office at Weissensee and kept a tape running? It seemed obvious now, even if it hadn't seemed obvious then.

I wasn't quite convinced by this explanation, which shifted all responsibility for the report of the taxi journey to some shadowy figures in anoraks. Would the signal have been strong enough to reach all the way to Leipzig? And after all, there was still the report with Ruika's alias on it. Neumann must have had the same thought. Why did you file that pointless report then, he asked. Ruika said those reports were always pointless. The Stasi had approached him and wanted to find out what had happened, Ruika said, but he wasn't into it. Neumann looked pleased. That's it, we are done, he said. The operation was over, the rotten tooth had been pulled. Our evening at the Greek restaurant continued for another two hours, during which conversation finally flowed freely. Neumann and Ruika spoke about their university days, about Martin Luther and the poetry of Rilke, and discovered that they shared a love for welding. The magical thing about welding, Ruika said, was you couldn't see anything the first time you tried it, just blinding light. But at some point you learned to see through the light. It was hard to explain, Neumann agreed. There was a point when suddenly you could see very clearly how the metals started to flow into one another.

It was past midnight by the time we left, and a nightingale struck up somewhere in the trees nearby.

———————

On 7 January 1988, a report from Branch IX, the arm of the Stasi responsible for investigations of political significance, landed on the desk of Erich Mielke, the Minister for State Security. It detailed proceedings at a literary event inside the Zionskirche church in Berlin's Prenzlauer Berg district, four days before Christmas Eve. The Stasi had tried to prevent the event from taking place by sealing the front door, but one of the invited writers, Gert Neumann, had been able to open the back door to the church hall thanks to his training as a locksmith.

According to an unofficial collaborator present among the audience, the event was 'poorly attended', with no more than fifty people, some of whom left before the end. 'The reason for this was probably the poor acoustic conditions, but also lack of interest in Neumann's texts,' said the report. The author had brought along photographs of dilapidated buildings in the inner city of Halle, which he handed out to be passed through the rows during the reading, because the organisers hadn't been able to procure a projector. The texts, the informant reported back, 'were so cryptic that even persons with a literary bias had trouble understanding them'. The author was informed of this in the ensuing discussion, 'but refused to accept it'. In the view of the source, the reading was 'not a success for Neumann'.

The report was filed away to gather dust in the Stasi archives in Berlin. Six months later, though, the matter was picked up again. A note from Stasi headquarters to the local branch in Marzahn: was the informant not supposed to have passed on some of his poems to the writer Neumann, to be considered for publication in one of his literary journals? 'Has the informal collaborator received any feedback on his works? If so, what kind?' East Germany's secret police, which was so easily terrified of poetry, craved artistic recognition. 'If there hasn't been a response,' the letter continued, 'is there a possibility of contacting the suspect with the aim of enquiring whether the poems were of use, or have potentially already been accepted?'

It took the informant's handler a month to reply. The request had been received and the handler suggested that the questions would be considered when the informant received his next instructions. Doing so could take some time, however. Unofficial collaborator 'Michael Lindner', resident in Hohen Neuendorf, could not be contacted until the autumn as he would be spending more time in Leipzig, with a view to re-enrolling at the Institute for Literature. Alexander Ruika, who once dreamt of waking the 'Giant of Murom' in order to unleash the mythical defender of Russia's ancient borders on traitorous scribblers, had been inspired once again to search for his true self and dig up his own navel. The Giant of Murom had gone back to sleep.

Lesson 11

BROKEN RHYME

*A form of rhyme, produced by dividing a word at the line
break of a poem to make a rhyme with the end word of
another line.*

The GDR had always taken pride in striding in lockstep with
the Soviet Union. In the brotherhood of Eastern Bloc satellite
states, it stood out amongst equals. Along with Bulgaria, it was
the only state in the bloc to write the alliance with Russia into its
constitution. East Germany's geographical location on the class
enemy's doorstep meant it took a special place in USSR military
planning. In return, it rarely took any political decision without
consulting Russia first. East Berlin was 'Moscow's model student',
as an article in *Die Zeit* had put it in 1974: 'No other state in the
Communist world has submitted itself so unconditionally to
Moscow's leadership claim.' But by the late 1980s, the centrifu-
gal forces of the Soviet Union were starting to change. In March
1985, fifty-four-year-old Mikhail Gorbachev was elected as the
new General Secretary of the Soviet Union's Communist Party,
and within months he admitted the unsayable: the USSR had
failed to stay abreast of world developments in science and technology, and the economies of the bloc were stagnating. In years
to come, Gorbachev's rule would become associated with two
concepts – *glasnost* ('transparency') and *perestroika* ('restructur-
ing') – but the first of his reform slogans was *uskoreniye*, meaning
'acceleration'. In order for the economy to accelerate, Gorbachev
soon realised, the state had to loosen the reins of the command

economy, allowing state enterprises to determine their output based on demand rather than centralised control.

Gorbachev stopped using the term *uskoreniye* after April 1988, but 'acceleration' was the right term to describe what the Soviet world in the last years of the 1980s looked like from the perspective of ordinary citizens. In Poland, the state reduced bureaucracy and allowed smaller private businesses to set up shop. After years of political repression, the Polish government invited the independent trade union, Solidarity, to join round-table negotiations in order to stave off strikes. Hungary relaxed restrictions for citizens wanting to travel to the West, culminating in the Hungarian and Austrian foreign ministers symbolically cutting down a barbed-wire fence in June 1989.

Only in East Germany was the government putting its foot on the brake and trying to cover its citizens' eyes and ears. Stasi chief Mielke was deeply sceptical of Gorbachev's reforms: he warned that they would not lead to a better socialism, but the wholesale abolition of socialism. Party newspaper *Neues Deutschland* took the highly unusual step of running an article defending Stalin against the new Russian reformists. From 1987, the East German government started censoring Russian publications; in November 1988, it stopped the distribution of the Soviet monthly *Sputnik*, after it ran articles on the German–Soviet non-aggression pact of 1939. If the centre of a universe is an unmoving celestial body that other bodies orbit, then the GDR was suddenly the sun of the Eastern Bloc: it was the only body that was not in motion. But for many of its citizens, the new world order was confusing, dizzying even. Rolf-Dieter Melis, a man the Stasi had once cherished for his cool head, wrote a poem called 'Stop Going Around in Circles'.

Don't you get yourself in a spin
Tender words need whisperin'
Speak up if you want to be heard
But never speak up to hurt.
And when no hope is in sight,
You can knock on my door late at night.

The second verse starts out like a blues lament, but the repetition creates a lyrical whirligig: thoughts are buzzing around Melis's head in ever tighter circles.

Sometimes you are strong, and sometimes weak
Sometimes you are tired, sometimes awake
Sometimes you are brave and don't know no harm
Sometimes a single word has the strength to disarm.
Sometimes the hottest summer day leaves you cold
Sometimes you grasp a spiders' web for hold

Blues songs are about loss and despair: 'The thrill is gone / It's gone away for good,' wails B. B. King. But they tend to end on a flick of redemption, a glimmer of hope in the act of voicing their grief: 'You know, I'm free, free now baby / I'm free from your spell.' But Rolf-Dieter Melis's poem is about a terror that dare not speak its name. The poem ends on a positive note that is even more unsettling because we know its optimism is fake:

And yet you carry on and pretend
That you are happy inside and always content.

I found Melis's *uskoreniye* blues in a cache of poems that Uwe
Berger had started to compile for an anthology to commemorate
the GDR's fortieth anniversary in 1989, with the working title *Man,
Soldier, Communist: Poetry and Prose by Writing Chekists*. The
booklet was due to be the fourth anthology of works produced by
the Stasi poetry circle, following 1969's prosaically titled *POEMS
by the Circle of 'Writing Chekists' and other Comrades of the Guards
Regiment Feliks Dzerzhinsky*, 1975's *I Met Dzerzhinsky . . . Chekists
Write for Chekists*, and the little red booklet that had first set me
off on my quest, 1984's *We About Us*. But finding the right poems
for the GDR's fortieth anniversary had evidently turned into a
struggle. The cache was full of loose pages that looked like they
had been shuffled and reshuffled. The title of the anthology kept
on changing, with Berger eventually opting for one that sounded
like a gesture of defiance: *In My Raised Fist*. Pages full of poems
were cut, including Rolf-Dieter Melis's blues. As a replacement,
Berger picked a poem called 'Letter of Recruitment':

> We are Dzerzhinsky's men
> To us our mission is clear
> ready to rise once again
> ready to fight with no fear.

It wasn't only the thoughts racing around Rolf-Dieter Melis's head
that were accelerating, but also the number of people leaving East
Germany. Around three million people had left the GDR between
its foundation and the year 1961, but the Wall, and fear of the snip-
ers, spring-guns and the dogs who guarded it, had been effective

in turning the stream into a trickle. Yet in the mid-1980s the numbers began to rise again. Some 21,500 citizens applied to leave the country in 1980. That number more than doubled five years later, to 50,600. Even though there was still no real legal basis for these 'applications for departure', the state granted 29,800 permissions in 1984, more than in the four previous years combined. This did not mean the state was not deeply concerned about what was going on. An analysis of the professional profile of the typical leaver made clear the GDR was facing a drain not just in numbers, but in brainpower too: as many as eighty-six per cent of them were under forty, most of them skilled workers and many with university degrees.

What could the East German state do to stop West Germany from cherry-picking its best and brightest? Gerd Knauer's Department for Agitation was called upon to somehow plug the gaps in the leaky border, even though it was itself in the process of being turned upside down: having been conceived as a relatively autonomous unit with the strategic role of proactively shaping Eastern Germans' view of the West, the Department for Agitation was being subsumed into the Central Analysis and Information Group, the ZAIG, where the Ministry could keep its propagandists on a shorter lead. Its new mission was a glorified exercise in public relations: selling the state apparatus, including the Stasi, back to the GDR's citizens. In the middle of this period of strategic realignment, the Department for Agitation was tasked with conceiving a large-scale campaign that would at the very least make people think twice about leaving the country. On 6 March 1985, loyal Party newspaper *Neues Deutschland* printed the headline '20,000 ex-citizens want to come back', and gave over a full page to 136 case studies of former East Germans who were disappointed with life under capitalism in the West. Engineer-economist Norbert Schrein, aged forty, said one of the entries, 'realised too late that in the GDR he was living in social security and comfort'. Many confessed to having been 'bedazzled' by West German television. Contrary to what many a cynic reading these accounts may think, the people behind them and their frustrations were real. The headline figure, though, was not: it was not twenty thousand ex-East Germans who applied to be let back in to their former country between January 1984 and December 1986, but a mere 719. Even of the 136 genuine case studies retold in *Neues Deutschland*, 103 had their application for re-entry rejected by the East German state. And even as fake news, the propaganda effort wasn't much of a success: the story of the wannabe returnees didn't even get a look-in among the thirteen headlines printed on *Neues Deutschland*'s tightly packed front page.

One explanation for why the GDR remained wedded to dogma while other Eastern states started to reform is that East Germany had always believed in the romantic idea of socialism with more heart and soul than the rest of the bloc, in an ideological fervour borne of a will to distance themselves wholly from Germany's brutal Nazi past. The events of 1988 and 1989 seemed to confirm that assumption. When the turning of the tide became undeniable, in the eleventh hour, it didn't feel like a change of mind, an argument winning over a majority, but an emotional emergency. When reformists started to speak up in the last years of the decade, it came with the sound of heartbreak. In May 1988, the bi-monthly literary journal *Sinn und Form* published a remarkable essay by its long-dead founding editor Johannes R. Becher, which read at first more like a mourning lover announcing the end of a relationship than the political provocation it was. 'I adored this man like no other amongst the living,' writes Becher. 'This veneration found expression in my poetry, and numerous of my verses give expression to what I loved and admired about him.' The object of this doomed affection was Josef Stalin and the essay, written in 1956 but purged from Becher's magnum opus *The Poetic Principle* by the author himself, was called 'Self-Censorship'. In the wake of Stalin's death, Becher had learnt about the late leader's bloody purges against political rivals and his ethnic cleansing of minorities in the Soviet Union, and chided himself for not having spoken up earlier: 'I can't excuse myself by saying I didn't know. I didn't just have a hunch, oh, I knew!' The man who had gloriously liberated East Germany from barbaric Nazi rule had himself been the perpetrator of barbaric crimes against humanity: that was one of the paradoxes that Becher could not dissolve even with the method of dialectical materialism. 'The biggest mistake in my life was the belief that socialism would end all human tragedy,' he wrote. 'It is more as if with the socialist system we are seeing the beginning of a new form of human tragedy, a kind previously unpredicted and still unforeseeable in its true extent.' The end of a long-term relationship can trigger the start of a painful process of re-evaluation, as one sifts through the honeymoon years for early signs of disharmony. In East Germany's case, that process had started in the 1950s, but only now, at the end of the 1980s, was it at last finding its voice.

––––––––––

At the start of 1989, the average age of the East German politburo was sixty-seven. Erich Mielke, the head of the Stasi, was eighty-one. Erich Honecker, the General Secretary of the Socialist Unity Party, was seventy-five, and like the rest of his gerontocracy, he was showing no sign of gracefully bowing out. The Socialist

Unity Party's failure to rejuvenate itself by filling key posts with younger members turned out out to be fatal for the state's stability in a moment of crisis. As the Soviet universe span ever faster, East Germany's political leaders started to feel dizzy. Honecker, suffering from biliary colic, collapsed at the summit in Bucharest on 7 July 1989 at which the Soviet Union officially annulled the 'Brezhnev doctrine', the USSR's commitment to intervene in the domestic affairs of Eastern Bloc countries when it saw socialist hegemony under threat. Just as the Soviet Union announced that the states of the Warsaw Pact now had the 'freedom to vote', East Germany was effectively without a leader. During Honecker's operation at Berlin's government hospital, doctors found a tumour on his kidney but dared not inform the General Secretary of their discovery. By the time the leader emerged from his sickbed on 26 September, the country was in turmoil. That same week, between four and eight thousand marchers took to the streets of Leipzig, chanting *Wir sind das Volk*, 'We are the people'. Later that chant would change to *Wir sind ein Volk* – 'We are one people' – but in autumn 1989 the idea that East and West Germany should be reunited as one country was still a minority view. Instead, most of the protesters were calling for sweeping political reforms that would nonetheless retain the country's commitment to socialism; they demanded the abolition of the Ministry for State Security and freedom for East German citizens to travel to the West. In the coming weeks, the number of demonstrators attending the 'Monday marches' kept growing, as did the number of people who voted with their feet in a different manner. On the border between Hungary and Austria, the Iron Curtain had sprung a leak, and throughout the summer East Germans had been pouring into the West in droves. The Stasi's Department for Agitation thought up another ruse: in national newspapers, it placed an interview with a young chef who said he had somehow ended up in the West German embassy in Vienna after a man at Budapest station had offered him a menthol cigarette spiked with chloroform: behind the mass exodus to the West, the article was meant to show, were ruthless people-smuggling capitalists. But the interview was widely ridiculed; *Neues Deutschland* was swamped with letters from readers who identified the story as a fabrication. In October, the month in which Honecker finally announced he was stepping down from his post for health reasons, another fifty-seven thousand left the country: had they all been drugged with menthol cigarettes?

Given that the East German state had invested so much time and effort in trying to nail down the ambiguities of the German language, it was only appropriate that when the final collapse came, it would not only be accompanied but directly brought about by words that said more than they were meant to say. At the start of November, the politburo decided that one way to navigate through the crisis was to communicate its decisions via Western-style press conferences, commenting on unfolding events in real time rather than by dictating official summaries of decisions made. It appointed Günter Schabowski, a former *Neues Deutschland* editor, as its first-ever spokesperson. At 6 p.m. on 9 November, Schabowski held his second-ever press conference along this new model inside a hot and stuffy room at the International Press Centre on Mohrenstrasse in central Berlin. The Socialist Unity Party was weighing up two possible measures to stop the mass exodus and quell brewing unrest: closing down all of its borders completely, which would risk pushing the country to the brink of civil war, or partially opening the border for people who wanted to leave the country permanently, thus getting rid of the biggest troublemakers. It opted for the latter: the plan was to briefly open the valve to release some pressure, then close it again straight afterwards. Schabowski, who had been booed and jeered relentlessly at a public event on Alexanderplatz a few days previously, made the most of being able to speak without interruption and talked for an hour. Some journalists in the overheated room started falling asleep. Then Riccardo Ehrman, a correspondent for the Italian wire agency, ANSA, enquired about the new travel restrictions for East German citizens – earlier in the day, he had received a phone call from a friend working at the GDR state broadcaster, suggesting he ask a question on the subject. Schabowski responded by reading out the new regulations that would allow people to travel westwards – the words 'temporary, transitional' had been dropped from the text he was holding in his hands because politburo members thought the prospect of free movement being immediately revoked again could provoke civil rights activists. A question from the audience: when would these new rules come into effect? Schabowski, peering at his notes through frameless glasses, fumbled for words: 'That is . . . as far as I am aware . . . it is right now, immediately.' Schabowski might have deliberately left his announcement right until the end of the press conference, but he hadn't foreseen the consequences that two of his words, 'right now', would have. The politburo had planned only to announce the new border rules on East German radio at 4 a.m. the following day; border guards across Berlin had not yet been issued with new guidelines. But by 7.03 p.m. the first news wires reported that the border was effectively open. By 8.30, thousands of East Berliners had gathered at the Bornholmer Strasse crossing, where the Prenzlauer Berg and Pankow districts bordered on the West Berlin district of Wedding. At 10.30 p.m., border guards raised the barriers. At 10.42, West German television announced that 'the gates of the Wall are wide open'.

The East German regime's power players, who had spent so much time worrying about the written word, were now struggling for words that could describe what was happening in front of their eyes. Four days after the borders opened, there was a meeting of the People's Chamber, East Germany's parliament, which was notionally made up of delegates from ten different parties but had in the past merely rubber-stamped decisions taken by the Socialist Unity Party. But on 13 November, after the politburo had already announced its formal resignation, the atmosphere in the People's Chamber was different. Towards the end of the session, Stasi head Erich Mielke asked to speak in the chamber, for the first time in his career. He didn't have a script in front of him, but he wanted to defend his Ministry for State Security: they had seen the latest escalation coming for a long time, and their warnings had been ignored again and again. Trying to appeal for the delegates' sympathy, he repeatedly used the term 'comrades' – and was suddenly rebuked. 'There are not only comrades in this chamber,' one delegate answered him back. Mielke was flustered. The politburo was not used to being cut off. 'Please, surely that's only a question of formalities,' Mielke said. There were jeers from the chamber. He tried to make light of the situation, and raised his arms: 'I love all . . .' Now there was laughter. 'I love all of humanity.' The laughter was deafening, and the confused man peering out from behind outmoded tortoiseshell glasses suddenly looked every one of his eighty-one years. In the context of Mielke's speech, his words were meant merely as a jocular excuse for using the term 'comrades', but language was slipping from the Stasi's grasp. The phrase 'I love all of humanity' immediately became part of national folklore: within a few months, it was the title of an anthology of dispatches from inside the Ministry for State Security, sold off the back of trucks stopping in the streets. To joking Berliners, the Stasi was now the 'Ministry of Love', the name of the most powerful ministry in George Orwell's *1984*.

———————

In *1984*, the Ministry of Love is also known as 'the place where there is no darkness', because the lights in its headquarters burn throughout the night. On almost any night of the past forty years, this would also have been an apt description of the Stasi headquarters on Ruschestrasse, in Berlin's Lichtenberg district. But on the night of 14 January 1990, for the first time in the history of East Germany's secret police, the headquarters of its mass surveillance programme were shrouded in black. Only the sound of a radio, audible through an open window in the inner courtyard, gave away that some people were still hard at work propping up the collapsing political regime and its intelligence agency: Gerd Knauer was one of them. He sent me his diary entry from that night. He recalls a song wafting across the courtyard: Kaoma's 'Lambada', the previous year's big Brazilian summer smash. *Chorando estará ao lembrar de um amor / Que um dia não soube cuidar*, the Portuguese lyrics went. 'He will be crying, to remember a love / that one day he didn't know how to care for.'

The Chekist flame had burnt through its wick. A big demonstration at the Soviet war memorial in November had failed to rally the nation behind the Stasi. Two weeks after this show of solidarity at Treptower Park, the GDR's Council of Ministers had renamed the secret police the Office for National Security, but the new body didn't even last a month: on 8 December 1989, the new East German Prime Minister, Hans Modrow, ordered its dissolution. District offices had already been wound down after protesters forced their way into Stasi buildings in Erfurt, Suhl, Schwerin and Leipzig, shouting 'We want to see our file' to the tune of the popular Bavarian-dialect ditty *Ja, wir san mit'm Radl da* ('Yes, we've turned up on our bikes'). If there was still a flicker of hope in the blacked-out rooms of the headquarters on Ruschestrasse, it was because some thought the Stasi could still be reformed by dividing it along the model of Western intelligence agencies, with one body focusing on foreign espionage while the other was solely dedicated to 'protecting the constitution'.

But public opinion was blowing in the other direction, and in the dying days of the GDR the public was hard to contain. On 14 January 1990, citizens' committees had announced a protest outside the Ruschestrasse headquarters at 5 p.m., and thousands of ordinary Berliners answered their call. Many of them brought bricks and mortar, to symbolically seal up the entrance to the home of the hated agency. In flyers and on placards, they called for the Stasi's immediate dissolution, a stop to all plans to form a successor agency, and for all its employees to be barred from entering the buildings where the Ministry's archives were held. The suspicion was that the old guard was deliberately slowing down negotiations with the citizens' committees in order to win time to destroy records that could incriminate key figures in the old system. Their fears were not entirely unfounded: for the last few weeks, remaining Stasi employees had been queueing up across the courtyard to access the cellar behind Haus 2, where a green mill was working day and night to mix paper files and water into a mush. Shredders were worked until they broke down. Some rooms were filled to the roof with intelligence confetti.

That day, most of the Stasi's employees had already left the building by 3 p.m., to avoid provoking the protesters. But a number of higher-ranking officers were still inside, sitting in darkened rooms. Willi Opitz, the head of the Stasi academy, had suggested they move their desks into rooms facing the courtyard, and that staff cars should not be parked in the streets outside the headquarters. 'You have to think of the optics,' he said. Members of the Feliks Dzerzhinsky Guards Regiment had been ordered to guard the building and prepare for the national emergency their unit was set up for. Last-ditch hopes had rested on the weather forecast: perhaps icy roads would keep the number of protesters down. But by late afternoon it was clear that the winter of 1989–90 would continue to be a mild one. Some Stasi officers suggested diluting the demonstration outside the gate by infiltrating it with young soldiers, but the plan was short-lived: it soon became clear that the crowd was simply too large.

Knauer started brewing coffee in the head of department's office in Haus 4 at 6 o'clock in the evening: him and his colleagues were bracing themselves for a long night. On the way to work, he had seen a poster with the slogan *Mit Fantasie gegen Stasi und Nasi,* calling on protesters to use 'imagination against Stasi and Nasi', the abbreviation for the new National Security agency. Over-confident on matters lyrical to the last, Knauer couldn't stop himself thinking that the slogan didn't really rhyme (the stress in *Fantasie* falls on the final syllable but on the a in Stasi). While the coffee machine was sputtering away, he fumbled around the dimly lit room for his cigarettes. Knauer's gaze fell through the back-facing window: around thirty people were standing in the inner courtyard. They weren't wearing uniforms. Some of them appeared agitated, zigzagging from one building to the next, rattling at the doors on the ground floor and pointing at the upper floors. Knauer realised that his building, Haus 4, was the only one with lights burning on the staircase. He slowly stepped back from the window.

Gerd Knauer's diary was less of a diary than a memoir, reflecting on the follies of the Stasi's leadership. He expresses his frustration with colleagues, most of whom had refused to pop over to the West even after the border crossings had opened: it was as if they feared that the very idea of an independent socialist East Germany would go up in smoke once they set foot on enemy territory. Knauer disagreed. He had written to his superiors to appeal against the Stasi's directive banning its employees from making any trips to the West. There were practical arguments against it: wouldn't it make it easier to identify members of the secret police in the future, by comparing the list of those who had claimed the 100 Deutsche Mark 'welcome money' on the other side of the Wall against the population of the GDR? And there was a point of principle: why should East Berliners not be allowed to cross over to the other side like their relatives in the West? Knauer himself had already made the trip to the forbidden land. Only a week after the fall of the Wall, curiosity had got the better of him and he'd walked into the American sector at Glienicker Brücke, where Eastern and Western intelligence agencies once used to exchange captured agents. In the West, politicians and commentators had started to claim that the Soviet Union was collapsing because it couldn't resist the lure of capitalism in all its garish technicolor, its sickly sweet tastes and smells. But when Knauer finally crossed over to the

West with a thumping heart and bought himself a can of West German beer at a petrol station, the taste couldn't have been more underwhelming: capitalism tasted watery. The lure of the West, he realised, was also of the East's own making. Capitalism wasn't beautiful enough to be banned.

The lights on the staircase were shining bright, too bright. If the protesters stormed the building, Knauer and his colleagues began to worry, they would be able to seek them out like moths to a flame. They wandered around the building for fifteen minutes, trying to find a switch to turn off the lights on the staircase. By the time they gave up, their coffee had gone cold. Knauer lit a match and walked through the open fire door from Haus 4 into Haus 2. He could hear the protesters chant: 'Out with the Stasi' and 'Hang the Stasi pigs'. Something about those chants sounded different now. Then he realised why. The chants were coming from inside the building. Knauer hurried back, locked the door from the inside, switched off the remaining lights and the TV. He and his colleagues peered through the closed blinds. What did these people want, one of them whispered. Knauer wondered if they'd rather be down there with them, protesting against the failures of their own government. Someone pressed down the door handle of their room. Once tentatively, then again with force. One of Knauer's colleagues resignedly slumped into his chair, whispering: if they find us, they are not going to waste any time asking questions. They counted the number of times someone tried to open their door: fifteen attempts in the space of an hour, then the rattling stopped.

Around 9.30 p.m., the group dared switch on the television set, to find East Germany's main news programme broadcasting live from the complex of buildings they were in. A strange sense of calm spread around the room: it was as if they were no longer historical actors, but characters in a film. They learned that the broadcasters had followed the demonstrators who stormed Haus 18, which contained a hairdressing salon, a bookshop and a supermarket in which Stasi employees could purchase all sorts of Western goods inaccessible to ordinary citizens. Some protesters had broken into one of the archives and made a show of emptying them into the courtyard: sheets of A4 were raining from the sky. Knauer remembered that the files stored in Haus 18 were largely irrelevant – most of them were just holiday requests from Stasi employees – and wondered if some Stasi agents had managed to infiltrate the stream of protesters and direct them to the wrong building. Perhaps this wasn't the last night of East Germany's secret police after all.

Knauer had spent the previous weeks hatching plans. He was trying to work out if there was a way in which the reputation of the Stasi could be saved, if it committed itself outright to a reform programme. His hope was that a figure with both knowledge of the secret police's inner machinations and credibility as a critical thinker, perhaps 'super spy' Markus Wolf, would be installed at the top of the agency. But Wolf had kept his head below the parapet. Knauer took pen to paper and wrote himself into a rage. He composed a seven-point plan. The Stasi had to go on a final public relations offensive, at last showcasing some of the more useful and harmless work it had done, exposing conditions to which the ministries had turned a blind eye, such as the poor state of the motorways or the lack of equipment in hospitals. It had to get rid of the old Stalinist blowhards and fire corrupt officers, agree to regular press conferences and proper parliamentary oversight. Now was the time to nail your flag to the mast of a truly humane, truly democratic socialism. He had shown his manifesto to a friend and colleague, who had quickly locked it in a safe, to save him from getting into trouble. As Knauer pondered how the East German dream could be kept alive, the TV suddenly cut to a shot inside the foyer of Stasi HQ. The scene that flashed up for a few seconds on the grainy screen was easily missed. But it was enough to dispel any remaining illusions the confident young officer harboured about the future of the state he served.

East Germany goes down in history for the infamous distinction of having endured two different dictatorships on its soil within the space of a century. Calling the GDR a dictatorship is indisputable – even if, as the British historian Richard J. Evans has argued, its 'German' character can be questioned with view to Moscow's control over Berlin. This is not to say these two dictatorships were essentially the same. The Third Reich ended with a genocide of six million Jews and five million other persecuted victims. The GDR ended with an uprising that remained bloodless: there were no burnt bodies, only pulped files. Nazi Germany radicalised itself until it went up in flames, with fervent supporters of a fascist regime fighting on even when their cause was lost: East Germany drained itself of hope, with Stasi officers resignedly watching their own demise on a television screen. But it did leave behind a heap of broken promises, some of which were specifically cultural. The promise that a country could learn from its immediate history and build a new state around its literary heritage. The promise that high literacy will necessarily bring out the best in us. And the promise that politics could be trusted to respect culture as an equal, 'a great sovereign power' in Becher's turn of phrase, instead of co-opting it for its own ends.

The picture on the TV set around which Knauer and his colleagues had gathered was a wry comment on this state of affairs.

It showed the bottom of the staircase in Haus 18 of the Stasi headquarters, next to which stood a glass vitrine displaying artistic works by Stasi employees: clay sculptures, oil paintings, and some poems produced by the Stasi poetry circle, including Gerd Knauer's own verses. *Einblick in unser Volkskunstschaffen* was written in white paint on a beige plaque: 'A Peek at our People's Art'. But overnight the glass of the vitrine had been smashed. Some prankster had crossed out a couple of letters. *VOLKSKUNSTSCHAFFEN* had become *VOLKSUNSCHAFFEN*: 'The People's Art' was now 'The People's Mis-accomplishments'. Somewhere behind him, Knauer could hear a voice, muttering to itself: 'Those vandals.'

Lesson 12

EPITAPH

A form of words written in memory of a person who has died, especially on a tombstone.

Three weeks after the storming of the Stasi headquarters, East Germany's government gave orders that its secret police should be dissolved by 31 March 1990. By then, East Germany's first free elections for the People's Chamber had been won by the Alliance for Germany, made up of the Christian Democratic Union, the German Social Union and Democratic Awakening – the spokesperson for the latter was a young chemist called Angela Merkel, who had throughout the previous decade worked at the Central Institute for Physical Chemistry across the road from the Guards Regiment. On 22 August, the People's Chamber voted for the GDR to sign up to the constitution of the Federal Republic of Germany. East Germany was no more.

A printing permission for the Circle of Writing Chekists' last anthology was issued on 31 December 1989. But it never made its way to the printers. In the final manuscript, the original title *Writing Chekists* is crossed out and updated with the correct new name for their employers: *Lyrical Circle in the Office for National Security*. A dedication to the fortieth anniversary of the foundation of the GDR and the Ministry for State Security is also crossed out: the anthology now merely bears witness to the 'thoughts and feelings, motivation and deeds of our time and our struggle, to the love of our socialist homeland and the solidarity with the workers in our country'.

Jürgen Polinske worked as an archivist at Berlin's Humboldt University from 1990 until his retirement in 2018. For the last fifteen years of his employment, the job involved looking after the university's science collection, which is held in an outpost in Adlershof, less than a hundred metres from where the Stasi poetry circle used to meet. The Feliks Dzerzhinsky Guards Regiment's Culture House has been torn down; some of the former barracks now house a job centre, the *Agentur für Arbeit*. Polinske still writes his own verse, and runs a poetry circle in Adlershof.

Uwe Berger's publisher informed him three months after the fall of the Berlin Wall that they would allow his contract to expire the following month. His request for a reissue of his 1987 memoirs, showing his 'turn to perestroika', went unanswered. In 2006, *Der Spiegel* confronted Berger with the reports showing that he had spied on his students at the Stasi poetry circle. 'From a contemporary standpoint I cannot explain my behaviour, nor make excuses for it,' he told his interviewer. 'I ask those affected for forgiveness.' In his diaries, self-published as an e-book in 2013, Berger complained that the resulting article was 'one-sided' and noted that West Germany's domestic intelligence agency, the BND, had also tried to gather information on *Der Spiegel*: 'No intelligence agency can do without so-called reports.' Two years after his death in February 2014, a new poetry prize in Uwe Berger's name was to be set up at a literature festival in Berlin's Köpenick district. The prize was renamed following objections by Berger's former colleagues and contemporaries from the East German literary scene.

———————

Björn Vogel works as a caretaker and a private driver for hire. On his Facebook page, he shares YouTube videos arguing that the Covid-19 pandemic is a ploy to prop up ailing Western economies and establish a dictatorship of global elites.

———————

After Rolf-Dieter Melis's death, Hilde finished building the house in Königs-Wusterhausen on her own and still lives there today. She says she misses the good old GDR.

———————

Annegret Gollin still works as a tour guide at the German Chancellery. After retirement, she will receive a monthly state pension of 414 euros and compensation of 300 euros a month for East Germans who spent more than 180 days in prison, but because the GDR systematically denied her regular employment it is unclear if she can draw further state support that she would otherwise have been eligible for. Her monthly living costs are around 1,000 euros. The German state still pays the pensions of former Stasi employees, on average around 1,400 euros a month. Annegret Gollin no longer writes poetry.

———————

Gerd Knauer has changed his name and works as a tax adviser. Some of his clients used to be senior officers in the Stasi. After reunification Knauer wrote three crime novels under the pseudonym Max Adam, which were published in the same years as the first three books in Henning Mankell's Wallander series, though with less commercial success. He is working on his memoirs.

———————————

Gert Neumann has moved to Wittenberg, to spend more time studying Martin Luther.

———————————

Alexander Ruika never completed his literature degree. After the fall of the Wall, he worked as a detective at a department store, then as private security for a German recycling tycoon, and eventually set up his own agency offering security and surveillance services. He is now retired, and spends his time repairing vintage motorbikes and occasionally writing poems.

SOURCES

Adam, Max D., *Yeti sei tot* (Das Neue Berlin, 1992)

Arendt, Hannah, *The Origins of Totalitarianism* (Penguin Classics, 2017)

Arndt, Erwin, *Deutsche Verslehre* (Gondrom, 1989)

Bailey, James, and Tatyana Ivanova, *An Anthology of Russian Folk Epics* (M. E. Sharpe, 1999)

Baumann, Christiane, *Das Literaturzentrum Neubrandenburg 1971–2005* (Robert-Havemann-Gesellschaft, 2006)

Bittorf, Wilhelm, 'Nun erfüllt sich der bittere Rest', in *Der Spiegel*, 5 February 1984

Becher, Johannes R., 'Das poetische Prinzip', in *Bemühungen II* (Aufbau, 1971)

—— 'Macht der Poesie', in *Bemühungen II* (Aufbau, 1971)

—— 'Selbstzensur', in *Sinn und Form*, May 1988

Berger, Uwe, *Der Schamanenstein* (Aufbau, 1980)

—— *Die Neigung* (Aufbau, 1984)

—— *Pfade hinaus: Episoden der Erinnerung* (Mauer, 2005)

—— *Ungesagtem lauschen: Aus dem Tagebuch der Jahre 2000 bis 2012* (Edition digital, 2013)

—— *Weg in den Herbst* (Aufbau, 1987)

Bergmann, Christian, *Die Sprache der Stasi* (Vandenhoeck & Ruprecht, 1999)

Budek, Josef, *Arbeit am Feind* (Astak Verlag, 2007)

Decker, Gunnar, *1965: Der kurze Sommer der DDR*
(Bundeszentrale für politische Bildung, 2015)

Dobrenko, Evgeny and Natalia Jonsson-Skradol (eds), *Socialist Realism in Central and Eastern European Literatures Under Stalin* (Anthem Press, 2018)

Doward, Jamie, 'How a Nato war game took the world to the brink of nuclear disaster', in the *Observer*, 2 November 2013

Dwars, Jens-Fietje, *Johannes R. Becher: Triumph und Verfall: Eine Biographie* (Aufbau, 2003)

Emmerich, Wolfgang, *Kleine Literaturgeschichte der DDR* (Kiepenheuer, 1996)

—— *Seven Types of Ambiguity* (New Directions, 1966)

Fedor, Julie, *Russia and the Cult of State Security: The Chekist Tradition, From Lenin to Putin* (Routledge, 2013)

Fühmann, Franz, *Die dampfenden Hälse der Pferde im Turm von Babel* (Hinstorff, 2005)

Geary, James, *I Is an Other: The Secret Life of Metaphor and How It Shapes the Way We See the World* (Harper Perennial, 2012)

Gieseke, Jens, *Die Stasi 1945–1990* (Pantheon, 2011)

—— *Die DDR-Staatssicherheit: Schild und Schwert der Partei* (Bundeszentrale für politische Bildung, 2001)

Gollin, Annegret, *Deutschland – ein Lügenmärchen* (Labyrinth, 1990)

—— *Doppelbelichtung* (Wilfried Bonsack, 1996)

Gorky, Maxim, *V.I. Lenin* (Lenin Museum and Maxim Gorky Internet Archive, 2002)

Haffenden, John (ed.), *Selected Letters of William Empson* (Oxford University Press, 2006)

Hänisch, Werner, and others, *Kleines politisches Wörterbuch* (Dietz, 1988)

Heidemarie Härtl, *Puppe im Sommer* (Edition Büchergilde, 2006)

Hecht, Jochen, 'Die Poesie als Magd des Staatssicherheitsdienstes', Beitrag für die Internationale DDR-Forschertagung in Weimar, November 2005

Herwig, Malte, *Die Flakhelfer: Wie aus Hitlers jüngsten Parteimitgliedern Deutschlands führende Demokraten wurden* (DVA, 2013)

Jones, Nate (ed.), 'The 1983 War Scare: "The Last Paroxysm" of the Cold War Part I' (National Security Archive Electronic Briefing Book No. 426)

Kirchner, Stephanie, 'Berlin Wall: Was the Fall Engineered by the GDR?', in *Time*, 19 April 2000

Knauer, Gerd, and others, *Wir über uns: Reprint einer Anthologie der Kreisarbeitsgemeinschaft 'Schreibende Tschekiste'* (Verlag Haus am Checkpoint Charlie, 1990)

Kowalczuk, Ilko-Sascha, *Endspiel: Die Revolution von 1989 in der DDR* (C.H. Beck, 2009)

Löffler. Dietrich, *Buch und Lesen in der DDR: Ein literatursoziologischer Rückblick* (Ch. Links, 2011)

Mayer, Wolfgang, *Flucht und Ausreise* (Anita Tykve Verlag, 2002)

Mittenzwei, Werner, *Die Intellektuellen* (Faber & Faber, 2001)

Neumann, Gert, *Die Schuld der Worte* (Hinstorff, 1989)

—— *Elf Uhr* (DuMont, 1999)

Pincus, Walter, Soviets' Posture Shifts as SS20s Deployed, in *The Washington Post*, 25 October 1983

Rebohle, Eberhard, *Rote Spiegel: Wachsoldaten in der DDR* (Das Neue Berlin, 2006)

Rosenthal, M. L., *Our Life in Poetry: Selected Essays & Reviews* (Persea Books, 1991)

Ruika-Franz, Viktoria, *Auf den Spuren der Kupferfee* (Verlag
   Junge Welt, 1980)
——— *Die Federkielhexe* (Der Kinderbuchverlag, 1989)
——— *Für das Grosssein hab ich Pläne* (Der Kinderbuchverlag, 1974)
Saunders, Frances Stonor, *Who Paid the Piper? The CIA and the
   Cultural Cold War* (Granta, 1999)
Sarotte, Mary Elise, *The Collapse: The Accidental Opening of the
   Berlin Wall* (Basic Books, 2014)
Töpelmann, Sigrid, *Autoren, Figuren, Entwicklungen: Zur
   erzählenden Literatur in der DDR* (Aufbau, 1975)
Joachim Walther: *Sicherungsbereich Literatur: Schriftsteller und
   Staatssicherheit in der Deutschen Demokratischen Republik*
   (Ch. Links, 1996)
Walther, Joachim, with Ines Geipel, *Gesperrte Ablage:
   Unterdrückte Literaturgeschichte in Ostdeutschland 1945–1989*
   (Lilienfeld Verlag, 2015)
Walther, Joachim, 'Die Firma schreibt vor und mit', in *Der Spiegel* 40,
   1996
Wolf, Friedrich, 'Die Gans und die Nachtigall', in *Du bleibe!* (Das
   Neue Berlin, 2003)
——— 'Gymnasten über Euch', in *Du bleibe!* (Das Neue Berlin,
   2003)
——— 'Kunst ist Waffe', in *Du bleibe!* (Das Neue Berlin, 2003)
——— *Maxim Gorki* (Henschelverlag, 1953)

PERMISSIONS CREDITS

Poems quoted in the book are copyright and reproduced with kind permission, as follows:

'Concretia' ('Betonien') and 'I Laugh at You' ('Ich lache euch aus')
© Annegret Gollin
'Summer' ('Sommer') and 'The Bang' ('Der Knall') © Gerd Knauer
'Come' ('Komm') © Jürgen Polinske
'At the Monument to the Red Riders of Lviv' ('Am Denkmal der Roten Reiter bei Lviv'); 'Spring Birds' ('Frühlingsvögel'); 'My Noble Family' ('Meine adlige Familie'); 'Disagreement over Orderliness' ('Ordnungsstreit'); 'Masks' ('Masken'); 'Workshop or Armoury' ('Werkstatt oder Zeughaus'); 'In My Power' ('In meiner Macht'); 'Seeking Power' ('Machtstreben'); 'Dreams' ('Träume'); 'I Tried to Be Friendly' ('Ich wollte freundlich sein'); 'Transformation in Autumn, or The Call-Up' ('Verwandlung im Herbst, oder Die Einberufung'); 'In Anger, or: After a Discussion about Literature' ('In Wut – oder nach einer Literaturdiskussion') © Alexander Ruika

In some cases it has not been practicable to fully acknowledge copyright of poems cited.

ACKNOWLEDGEMENTS

I am grateful to the people who gave up their time to be interviewed for this book. Some of them are part of the story: Annegret Gollin, Ulrich Grasnick, Gerd Knauer, Hilde Melis, Gert Neumann, Jürgen Polinske, Alexander Ruika, Eduard Scherner, Sigrid Töpelmann. Others shared their memories or expertise: Matthias Braun, Holger Brom, Christiane Baumann, Martina Dost, Astrid Köhler, Helmut Müller-Enbergs, Kathrin Schmidt, Philipp Springer. I owe thanks to Dagmar Hovestädt, Friedrich Rother, Hans-Jürgen Rother and Raphaela Schröder for guiding me through the Stasi archive, to Marcel Lepper and Gabriele Radecke at the Akademie der Künste's literature archive, to Frank Willmann for access to his private library of Chekist literature, to 'Bondologist' Martin D. Brown's encyclopaedic knowledge of the 007 canon, and to the Russian folklore expertise of Robert Chandler, Yuliya Komska, Marina Warner and Jan Zielinski.

I am grateful to Cornelia Saxe, who let me listen to her archived 2006 radio documentary, and to Malte Herwig, without whose article in *Der Spiegel* the story of the Stasi poetry circle would likely have passed me by completely. Thank you to Abul Choudhury and Caroline Tomlinson at Age UK Camden, whose work at the Great Croft Centre ended up influencing this book in ways I hadn't anticipated. Tom Gatti, Tom Smith, Craig Taylor, Sabine Rennefanz and Kevin Hilliard read first drafts of the book and provided invaluable feedback: I owe you all several lavish dinners. I am indebted to Walter Donohue at Faber and Peter Straus at RCW, who were incredibly supportive of the book when it was still the sketchiest of ideas, and to Paul Baillie-Lane for his patience in the editing process. Thank you to Sarah Bohn, to my parents and sisters for their relentless support, and to my sweet boy Ernest, who was born at the same time as this book. Last but not least, thank you to my wife and teammate Anna, for being this book's single most energetic champion, fiercest guardian of tight prose, and most righteous slayer of overwrought metaphors (apart from this one).

INDEX

Written works are listed under the name of the author/poet. Definite articles (The, Der, Die, Das) are ignored for the purpose of alphabetisation.

Also by Philip Oltermann

Keeping Up with the Germans

Inspired by his own experiences of both countries, Philip Oltermann looks at eight historical encounters between English and German people from the last two hundred years: Helmut Kohl tries to explain German cuisine to the Iron Lady, the Mini plays catch-up with the Volkswagen Beetle and Joe Strummer has an unlikely brush with the Baader-Meinhof gang.

'A highly entertaining and perceptive look at the relationship between our two great countries.' *Sunday Times*

'For those whose knowledge of German history is bookended by the Beer Hall putsch and the rubble of the Berlin bunker, there is much illuminating stuff.' *Financial Times*

'A wonderful, surprising book that will have you rethinking British life even if you never, ever, get the Germans.' *The Times*

faber

Keeping Up with the Germans

Faber